The Best Preaching on Earth

MONTREAT
COLLEGE

Mark T. Lassiter
Associate Professor Biology/Environmental Studies

BOX 1267 ■ MONTREAT, NORTH CAROLINA 28757
704 669 8012 EXT 3303 ■ FAX 704 669 9554
HOME 704 669 1833

The Best Preaching on Earth

Sermons on Caring for Creation

Edited by Stan L. LeQuire

Evangelical
Environmental
Network

Judson Press ® Valley Forge

The Best Preaching on Earth: Sermons on Caring for Creation
© 1996 Judson Press, Valley Forge, PA 19482-0851

Unless otherwise indicated, Scripture quotations in this volume are from HOLY BIBLE: *New International Version,* copyright © 1973, 1978, 1984. Used by permission of Zondervan Bible Publishers. Scripture quotations marked KJV are from *The Holy Bible,* King James Version. Scripture quotations marked NRSV are from the New Revised Standard Version of the Bible, copyright © 1989 by the Division of Christian Education of the National Council of the Churches of Christ in the United States of America. Used by permission. All rights reserved. Scripture quotations marked Phillips are from *The New Testament in Modern English,* Rev. Ed. Copyright © 1972. Used by permission of The Macmillan Company and Geoffrey Bles, Ltd. Scripture quotations marked RSV are from the Revised Standard Version of the Bible, copyright © 1946, 1952, 1971, by the Division of Christian Education of the National Council of the Churches of Christ in the U.S.A. Used by permission.

"Prayer, Praise, and Play" was adapted from the original as it appeared in Eugene H. Peterson, *Where Your Treasure Is,* © 1985 Eugene H. Peterson, Wm. B. Eerdmans Publishing Co. Used by permission of Alive Communications.

"Of Whales and Polar Bears" is from Philip Yancey's book, *Finding God in Unexpected Places,* © 1995 and reprinted with permission of the publisher, Moorings.

"The Good Earth" is adapted from a chapter in Paul Brand's book, *The Forever Feast,* published by Servant Publications and used with permission.

Library of Congress Cataloging-in-Publication Data
The best preaching on earth : sermons on caring for creation / edited by Stan L.
LeQuire.
   p. cm.
   Includes bibliographical references (p.).
   ISBN 0-8170-1239-7 (pbk. : alk. paper)
   1. Human ecology—Religious aspects—Christianity—Sermons.
I. LeQuire, Stan L.
BT695.5.B48 1996
261.8'362—dc20   96-10661

This book is printed on recycled paper. ♻

Printed in the U.S.A.

12 11 10 09 08 07 06 05 04 03 02 01 00 99 98 97 96
10 9 8 7 6 5 4 3 2 1

This volume is dedicated to all those
who have nurtured the love of creation
within our souls. For me, this happened in my
childhood through the loving attention of my parents,
Valerie Riley LeQuire and Donald Lloyd LeQuire.
I am deeply grateful for the side trips to swamps
while we were on vacation, the books,
even your willingness to share our home with bugs
in bottles and snakes in the garage.
You sacrificed, and it has been rewarded.

Contents

Part Three

Part Four

Part Five

Part Six

Contributors

Myron S. Augsburger is president emeritus of Eastern Mennonite University and past president of the Christian College Coalition. He has pastored churches in Florida, Virginia, and Washington, D.C., and has served as pastor of students at Eastern Mennonite College. Dr. Augsburger is the author of several books on evangelism and social concerns.

Michael L. Blaine is pastor of Park Avenue Baptist Church in El Dorado, Kansas. Blaine pastored five other churches before coming to Park Avenue and has been involved in clinical pastoral education.

Paul Brand is a well-known hand surgeon and leprosy specialist and a consultant to the World Health Organization. He is author and coauthor of several widely acclaimed books.

Calvin B. DeWitt is professor of environmental studies at the Institute for Environmental Studies, University of Wisconsin, Madison, and director of the Au Sable Institute of Environmental Studies in Mancelona, Michigan.

Kevin Graham Ford is currently a leadership consultant for Christian ministries. He has also served as the director of evangelism at the Community Presbyterian Church in Danville, California, and as evangelism specialist for InterVarsity Christian Fellowship. Kevin is the author of *Jesus for a New Generation* (IVP, 1995).

Sharon Gallagher is editor of *Radix* magazine and associate director and faculty member of New College, Berkeley, California. She was also a founding member of the Evangelical Women's Caucus.

Madeleine L'Engle is presently the librarian of the Cathedral of St. John the Divine in New York City and is author of such well-known works of fiction as *A Wrinkle in Time* and *A Swiftly-Tilting Planet*.

Stan L. LeQuire directs the Evangelical Environmental Network, a fellowship of Christians committed to caring for creation as part of their discipleship. He has served as the pastor of a Baptist church in Maine. In addition, he has been an associate pastor, church planter, and short-term missionary in Africa, Asia, and Europe.

Gordon MacDonald pastors Grace Chapel, a nondenominational church in Lexington, Massachusetts. He is the author of numerous books and is a popular conference speaker.

Karen Burton Mains is cofounder, with her husband David, of Chapel of the Air Ministries. They were recently awarded "Best Television Show" by the National Religious Broadcasters for their daily broadcast, "You Need to Know."

Bishop George D. McKinney Jr. is the founding pastor of St. Stephen's Church of God in Christ in San Diego, California. In addition, he is the bishop for southern California's Second Jurisdiction of the Church of God in Christ and the founding president of Charles H. Mason University.

Dwight Ozard is editor of *PRISM,* the magazine of Evangelicals for Social Action, and an adjunct faculty member at Eastern Baptist Seminary. He has served as the youth and young adult minister for the Metropolitan United Church in London, Ontario. He has also been a radio host, producer, and writer.

Earl F. Palmer currently serves as the pastor of the University Presbyterian Church in Seattle, Washington, which is his third pastorate. He has also been a minister of students and the pastor of an international congregation in Manila. He has authored numerous books.

Virginia Patterson is president of Pioneer Clubs and an elder at Immanuel Presbyterian Church, Warrenville, Illinois. She has served as an adjunct professor at Wheaton College, Gordon-Conwell Theological Seminary, Trinity Evangelical Divinity School, and Columbia International University.

Eugene H. Peterson is professor of spiritual theology at Regent College in Vancouver, British Columbia, Canada. He was founding pastor of Christ Our King Presbyterian Church in Bel Air, Maryland, where he served for twenty-nine years.

Bob Seiple is president of World Vision United States, an international relief and development organization. Before joining World Vision, he was president of Eastern College (St. Davids, Pennsylvania) and Eastern Baptist Theological Seminary (Wynnewood, Pennsylvania).

Ron Sider is professor of theology and culture at Eastern Baptist Theological Seminary in Wynnewood, Pennsylvania, and president of Evangelicals for Social Action. He is ordained in both the Mennonite and Brethren in Christ churches and was a longtime elder at Diamond Street Mennonite Church in Philadelphia.

J. Alfred Smith Sr. pastors the Allen Temple Baptist Church of Oakland, California. *Ebony* magazine has listed Smith as one of the fifteen greatest African American preachers in the United States. He is also a lecturer, author, and seminary professor.

Howard A. Snyder is Heisel Professor of Evangelization and Church Renewal at United Theological Seminary in Dayton, Ohio. He has served as a pastor in Chicàgo, Detroit, and Sao Paulo, Brazil; has taught in seminaries in the United States and Brazil; and is an ordained elder in the Ohio conference of the Free Methodist Church.

John R. W. Stott is rector emeritus of All Souls' Church, Langham Place, London. His many books include the classic *Basic Christianity.*

Harold Dean Trulear is dean of First Professional Programs and professor of church and society at New York Theological Seminary, and pastor of educational ministries at Community Baptist Church of Love in Paterson, New Jersey. He has served on pastoral staffs in several churches in New Jersey and Pennsylvania and spent ten years as an urban missionary for Youth for Christ/Campus Life.

Jim Wallis is the founding editor of *Sojourners* magazine. For years Jim has challenged Christians to engage in such issues as racism, economic justice, disarmament, and peacemaking among city gangs. Jim lives in the inner city of Washington, D.C.

Philip Yancey is the author of several award-winning books, such as *Where Is God When It Hurts?, Fearfully and Wonderfully Made,* and *Disappointment with God.* Yancey is also editor at large for the magazine *Christianity Today.*

Foreword

Gordon MacDonald

My grandmother MacDonald taught me to love the world. That is no small statement about a woman who was an intense student of the Bible, a strong advocate for world evangelization, and more passionately committed to a life of prayer than anyone I've ever known.

People like my grandmother are sometimes stereotyped as "enemies" of the world and culprits of the environmental decline. After all, they seem inordinately concerned about sin, about those to whom they refer as the "lost," and about how one convinces people to engage in greater spiritual discipline. So how do they have time to love the world?

Nevertheless, Grandmother MacDonald saw the world (the entire universe, in fact) as the platform upon which God stages a show of his glory. And one of her major aims in life was to discover that splendor in all the nooks and crannies of creation. For Grandmother, that meant that the glory of God existed in the city, in the sea, and in the countryside. And that was just the beginning.

When I was a child, she and I would walk through Brooklyn's

Prospect Park, laughing at the antics of monkeys and admiring the regal postures of the lions. We would hike the shoreline of Coney Island and take in the power of the ocean. At other times the trees and plants at Central Park's botanical gardens, the fish in its ponds, and the birds overhead were our entertainment. She reminded me at all times that the things we were seeing were God's gift, God's expression of his character, and God's artistry.

We would drink in all of this glory and much, much more, and my grandmother would say over and over again, "Son, always love this world; always love this world. God gave it; find his glory in the midst of it."

And so, under Grandmother MacDonald's tutoring, I learned a lifelong love for the world.

As I became more acquainted with theology, I began to realize that Grandmother had been teaching me one of the most fundamental truths of the Bible: God had created something out of nothing. That creation reflected a signal part of his nature: order, beauty, energy, growth. I saw that the world was a vast sanctuary where one, stimulated by his or her senses, could be caused to worship and behold a primary revelation of God the Creator.

In the last chapters of Job, God entered into a dialogue with the ancient sufferer. Job had asked some hard questions, and God responded with a tour of creation. Job was treated to a display of the heavenly bodies, the living things of the land, sea, and air. He witnessed the storms and the sunsets. In short, he was purposely overwhelmed by the glory of God in all the universe.

And then God asked this question: "Will the one who contends with the Almighty correct him?" (40:2). In other words, Job, what advice or counsel would you presume to offer the heavenly Creator? And Job, having been reduced to true size, can only answer: "I am unworthy—how can I reply to you? I put my hand over my mouth. I spoke once, but I have no answer—twice, but I will say no more" (40:4-5). Job was silenced by the glory of God.

But how does one have a Job-experience (that of being

silenced into reverential awe) if the creation has since been slowly and deliberately defiled through the greed and neglect of humankind? Can a cut and burned rain forest testify to the glory of God? Can a strip-mined mountain? a polluted river? Can an ocean speak of God's power if it is a dumping ground for nuclear or medical waste? Can water speak of God's purity and refreshment if it is mixed with spilled oil or other chemical toxins? And what of the blight of acid rain, untreated sewage, and manufactured objects (plastics and rubber goods) that will last a hundred thousand years in dumps and never degrade?

What shall we say of the degradation of the Siberian tundra? the creeping sands of the Sahara? the dying ponds throughout America's northeast? the fallen trees in Indonesia? the coal-drenched air of China and eastern Europe? the dwindling fish supply in the North Atlantic? and an atmosphere slowly warming toward a future catastrophe because of what we eject into the air each day?

If a world is treated like this, how can anyone claim to love it? In the future, how will our offspring see the glory that the Creator meant to embed in every cubic inch?

I grieve and repent over having lived through a period of history as part of a generation that has done more to cast a shadow over God's glory than any in the past. We have damaged what was not ours. And we have put what was supposed to be our grandchildren's creation inheritance in jeopardy. We did this because we were selfish, unthoughtful, and naive concerning the essence of stewardship. How will we answer for this one day?

In all of my Christian life, I have never heard any preacher in my tradition address these issues. I have heard much about the creation as it pertained to creationism. I sang "This World Is Not My Home, I'm Just A' Passing Through" with as much gusto as anyone. And I have continually been reminded that creation will all burn some day when Jesus comes. Did all of this become an unconscious pretext for remaining silent while we looted creation of its splendor?

So no one really pressed home to me the notion that respect

for the creation might just be a part of biblical stewardship, a unique way of assuring that the fundamental, evangelistic message of the God-who-is-there will be heard as the "heavens" declare his glory.

That is why I am glad to write an introduction to these sermons. Many of them are the sermons of people I call my friends, my brothers and sisters. They speak boldly, courageously, insightfully. And theirs is a message to be listened to carefully.

When our children were very small, my wife, Gail, and I took them on a canoe camping trip on the lakes of northern Quebec. A few days into the journey we came upon a small island and claimed it as our own for a few days. We were far into the wilderness. No one was around. But the evidence of past visitors was abundant. The island abounded in beer cans, plastic bottles, and assorted species of trash.

The second day of our stay, Gail suggested a novel project to the family: "Let's divide the island into four parts. And we'll each take a garbage bag and clean up all the trash. In this way, we'll give the island back to God, so that it will be beautiful once again, as he meant it to be."

In about two hours our small island was pristine once again. Several large garbage bags were filled with trash. Because we could not carry this much trash back to civilization, and because we were still in the era before "carry-out-what-you-carry-in" was popularized, we did the next best thing. We tied stones to the bags, took them to the middle of the lake, and sank them (my apologies to all strict environmentalists).

Back on shore we had a worship service. We "reconciled" the island back to its maker and rejoiced that we could once again witness the glory of God.

One of these sermons would have been helpful at that makeshift worship service. But perhaps what we did was a sermon in itself. Had she been there, Grandmother MacDonald would have been proud.

Acknowledgments

My personal thanks to all who have assisted in the creation of this resource, particularly the staff of the Evangelical Environmental Network and Evangelicals for Social Action. I would like to express my gratitude to Sharon Reives, Sheri Ozard, Terry Cooper, Cliff Benzel, and editorial assistants Jeron Frame and Lucas McBee. Special thanks to Ki Yub Sung for his dedicated labor of manually entering many of these sermons into the computer. Very special thanks to Mark Walden, whose editing skills, insights, and persistent contact with the preachers made this volume possible.

Introduction

Judah was thriving under the reign of King Josiah. Even though he was only eight years old when he ascended the throne, Josiah had made some radical departures from the godless ways of his predecessors. He worshiped Yahweh and was busy rebuilding the temple in Jerusalem when something even more radical occurred.

"Your Majesty, one of our priests, a Levite named Hilkiah, found this book while repairing the temple," said Shaphan, the royal secretary.

"Read it to me then," said Josiah. As regent, Josiah was a thoughtful twenty-six-year-old who thrived under the inspiration of new ideas.

After a few short paragraphs, Josiah became nauseated. Trembling, he stumbled from the throne and began clawing at his luxurious robes. His fingernails eventually snared a seam, and the king ripped the cloth in a ritually prescribed but heartfelt reaction to what he had heard.

Perhaps Josiah had expected stimulating philosophies or an inspiring collection of sermons from the priest, Hilkiah. This reading was supposed to ward off sleepiness during another boring afternoon. However, Josiah was listening to the revelation of Almighty God. Shaphan's lips were pronouncing the holy laws of Yahweh as recorded in the book of Deuteronomy.

It had been decades since these sacred words had been heard in Judah. Josiah had always reveled in his personal triumph of leading his kingdom far from the ways of his evil ancestors. But now, he saw exactly what Yahweh required of him. Josiah resolved to deepen his reforms. And thus he embarked on a new, invigorating spiritual journey that took Judah to new heights of righteousness.

In the following months, it seemed as if Josiah's zeal for reform knew no bounds. He read the Word—all of it—in the presence of the Israelites and personally renewed the terms of the covenant with Yahweh. His subjects were so inspired by his leadership that they followed his example and recommitted themselves to their covenantal obligations. Josiah roamed throughout his tiny kingdom, and with his personnel he sought out all idols and destroyed them. Many he ground into powder. Tossing the dust to dry desert winds, he prayed that his people would never return to such loathsome worship. Finally, the king put an end to all sacrifice of infants and children. In its place, another, more biblical ritual was reinstituted to recall a holy sacrifice: the Passover. Believe it or not, even something as foundational as the Passover had been forgotten in Judah for decades.

What a revival! Wouldn't any church welcome such a joyous renewal of spirit?

Josiah found a Book, and it brought revival. It is time for God's people in the last days of the twentieth century to rediscover the Word of God. Much of it we already know. We have devotional resources, study guides, and translations enough to fill up row upon row of shelves in the bookstore. Many of these are quite helpful. Nonetheless, it is my belief that large portions of Scripture are still hidden from God's people. These are the portions that deal with creation and its care. We all believe in creation. We know that God is the Creator of all things. However, usually it is only the preschool classes in our church schools that ever give creation more than a sidelong glance. Most of us can praise the Creator in our prayers but cannot say much more than, "Thanks for the sun and the cute flowers." Our Scriptures begin with creation and end with its redemption. It is one of the all-encompassing themes of the Bible. Yet, I would respectfully submit to you that this portion of the Bible may as well be buried in a time capsule underneath the cornerstone of your church and mine.

When will we retrieve this buried treasure? When will we be faithful to the *full* counsel of God?

The purpose of this volume is to bring about a renewed interest in the Word of God. Each sermon in this collection is designed to draw the people of God into a deeper relationship with the Creator God, to bring about much needed revival. This resource may also help challenge God's people to a deeper faithfulness to Christ. Can we really relax in our dedication and commitment when major portions of Scripture have been swept under the rug? This volume is dedicated to the Josiahs, the Shaphans, and the Hilkiahs who serve the church of Jesus Christ—the shepherds of God's sheep. May God inspire you with his creativity as you challenge your flock with the biblical mandate for the care of creation.

Rev. Stan L. LeQuire
Wynnewood, Pennsylvania
November 1995

Part One

Is Caring for Creation Really a Biblical Agenda?

If we believe in and know the Creator God, and we do, then shouldn't we above all people show the most concern about creation or, to use a secular term, the environment? If we desire with all of our hearts to honor God, how should we react when our fellow humans dishonor the handiworks of the Maker? If the creation forms a chorus of praise to the Creator, how should a Christian respond when singers disappear from the choir? Can we really claim that we want God to receive the highest praise, while we let creation's adoration fall quieter and quieter? If God calls creation "good," and even "very good" (Genesis 1:4,10,12,18,21,25,31), should a Christian show concern if that goodness is being degraded?

To care for creation as a Christian is thoroughly logical. To honor the Creator by taking a clear stand on behalf of creation makes a lot of sense.

Caring for creation is also deeply biblical.

And yet, many Christians hesitate to become involved in taking care of creation. For them, it just does not seem to be an area of legitimate Christian concern. The sermons in Part One help us start investigating the many texts that support a "biblical environmentalism." This investigation is a good beginning that many of the other sermons in this volume will further develop.

Deep Ecology, Deeper Theology takes a close look at the

biblical texts that reveal God's intentions for human life on the earth. Christians have often misinterpreted these passages from Genesis 1 and 2 to such a degree that the church needs a fresh look at the meaning of these two chapters, which form the foundation of biblical earth keeping.

Whoops! Biblical faith is not shy about miracles. There is room for plenty of them! One of the greatest is the fact that Jesus Christ took on created flesh and lived among us as one of us. The Incarnation has significant implications for creation care. Madeleine L'Engle shows us that creation is the arena for God's redeeming love, God's miraculous works, and even God's holy presence.

This Is My Father's World does a great service by calling our attention to the relevance of sin. Put simply, we have *sinned* in our treatment of creation. Bishop McKinney calls us to repentance and to justice.

The Balanced Life. The Ten Commandments are one of the foundations of our faith. Yet few of us have looked closely enough to notice that creation care appears in a significant way even there.

Tending the Garden without Worshiping It. Ron Sider believes strongly that environmentalists need to hear from Christians. He proposes four biblical principles that are crucial for the environmental movement and challenges us to live radically biblical lifestyles to remedy the crisis that faces us.

This World Is Not My Home? answers many questions that seem to arise from Scripture. Shouldn't we shun the world? Don't we have a heavenly home beyond this one? So why should we care about what is happening to our planet? Howard Snyder's bold answers to these questions move us toward confident creation care as supported by Scripture.

Deep Ecology, Deeper Theology

Michael L. Blaine

Text: Genesis 1 and 2

Our worship today coincides with the observance of the International Environmental Sabbath. We join with thousands of other Christians around the world to celebrate the majesty and grandeur of the created order. As we worship the author of creation, we reflect with awe on the glimpses of God revealed in the divine handiwork of the heavens and the earth. This is an opportunity for us to affirm our deepest respect for the creative grace behind our existence and to express our gratitude to the Creator for the beautiful world in which we live. We can also use this occasion to renew our commitment to treat the earth with the same reverence we give to all the mighty works of God.

Today's sermon title, "Deep Ecology, Deeper Theology," prompts me to share a story about the pastor of another church who delivered a series of sermons on some very "deep" issues. After preaching the third of these sermons, the minister retired as usual to greet people as they left the church. Soon, an elderly gentleman approached and shook hands with the preacher and then said, with a distinct gleam in his eye, "Reverend, you've preached some mighty deep sermons lately. If they get any deeper, we're all going to need chairs to stand on." Well, I hope it doesn't get quite that deep today!

My prayer is that we will constantly seek ways to deepen our appreciation for the world in which we live and for the God who made it—indeed, for the God who made us. One way to do this, undoubtedly the most enjoyable way, is to make it a habit to experience the glories of the creation firsthand.

Three years ago, our family had the opportunity to visit the Grand Canyon for the first time. I would recommend the experience to anyone; it so moved me that I was left speechless (a noteworthy event in the life of any preacher!). There is nothing quite like being in the presence of something so vast and grand that our minds struggle to comprehend it. At such times as these, God's presence seems indescribably real to me. It is then that I can understand why the psalmist declared, "The heavens are telling the glory of God; and the firmament proclaims his handiwork" (Psalm 19:1 RSV). The breadth and depth of creation are a magnificent inkling of the breadth and depth of the creative Spirit behind it.

As enjoyable as it may be to experience the majesty of God's world in person, we must also strive to deepen our understanding of both Creator and creation. We need to get beyond mere hikes and canoe trips, as enjoyable as these may be. As Christian people, we must make every effort to develop our spiritual lives and examine, in the light of Scripture, what we believe about this planet we call our home. This is our goal for today. I begin, though, by mentioning an event that happened more than two decades ago in the scientific discipline known as "ecology."

Deep Ecology

Ecology is the study of living organisms in their interdependence with one another and their interrelatedness to the world around them. Back in the early 1970s, an idea emerged in the science of ecology that challenged conventional ways of thinking about the world. The idea was so different that its originator proposed a new term to describe it. The phrase "deep ecology" was first used by a man named Arne Naess, who was a Norwegian philosopher, mountaineer, and former Nazi resister. For Naess, deep ecology suggested, among other things, that the natural world had an *intrinsic value* apart from any value that human beings might attach to it. Let that thought sink in for a few moments.

Until the advent of deep ecology, much of the environmental movement concerned itself with preserving nature for the use and enjoyment of present and future generations. In fact, this view was the impetus for the establishment of our first national parks in the early years of this century. For most people at that time, creation's value was extrinsic; it was rooted in its capacity to profit or please humankind. Thus many believed it was important to preserve large portions of the natural world for our benefit and the benefit of subsequent generations.

Arne Naess and other deep ecologists argued that the natural world had a basic value and worth irrespective of what we humans thought about it. Its *intrinsic* value came from within, not without. It was inherent. For the deep ecologist, the value of a tree is not that it puts oxygen into the air for humans to breathe, or that human beings can use it to build their homes and churches or can burn it to keep them warm in the winter. A tree's value is simply that it is a tree and is as much a vital part of the world as we are. This sort of thinking is truly radical and challenges thousands of years of human presumption and religious teaching about the natural world and our relationship with it.

Shallow Theology

For centuries many Christians presumed that God made the world primarily for human beings. They noted, after all, that Genesis 1:26 says God gave humanity *dominion* over much of creation, and countless people have taken this to mean the world is ours to do with as we please. The church firmly rooted much of its creation theology in this notion.

Let me share a passage taken from a commentary widely used in the early part of this century, *An Interpretation of the English Bible* by B. H. Carroll. Keep in mind that the Western world was still in the throes of the colonial feeding frenzy in this period of history. I quote from a section in the volume on Genesis that specifically addresses the *dominion* passage of Genesis 1:26.

In God's law neither man nor nation can hold title to land nor sea and let them remain undeveloped. . . . The ignorant savage cannot hold large territories of fertile land merely for a hunting ground. When the developer comes he must retire. . . . Mere priority of occupancy on a given territory cannot be a barrier to the progress of civilization. Wealth has no right to buy a county, or state, or continent and turn it into a deer park. *[Then comes the clincher.]* The earth is man's.

It may be hard for some of us to believe anyone could write such arrogant and selfish drivel, much less a Christian scholar, although he undoubtedly reflected the spirit of his time more than he ever shaped it. The truth is, we are still not far removed from this attitude and others like it that sanctioned the near genocide of the Native American peoples in the previous century. Such attitudes, I believe, continue to sustain numerous insidious practices. Such thinking has laid waste to the world's rain forests, polluted the air we breathe, poisoned the soil and the oceans, and driven countless life forms to the brink of extinction and beyond. It now threatens to unravel the very fabric of life on earth. Such a callous and shallow attitude, often pursued with the church's blessing, can hardly be what God intended. Clearly, it is time to put aside such shallow, and unbiblical, theology. We need to seek a new level of appreciation and a deeper understanding of what Scripture really teaches about creation. We need what might aptly be called a "deep theology."

Deep Theology

In our own time, many biblical scholars have rejected the traditional interpretation of *dominion* theology, stressing that we have greatly misunderstood and often distorted this biblical idea. At the very least, we must examine this traditional understanding in the context of the entire biblical record with an eye to the fullness and depth of biblical teaching. This approach can lead us to a deeper theology, that is, one that honors the Creator by respecting the creation.

I would suggest four biblical affirmations that can move us beyond the shallow theology of the past toward a deeper level of spiritual awareness and theological insight regarding God's world. These affirmations come from the books of Genesis and Psalms.

1. The first biblical affirmation significant for a deeper theology of creation comes from Psalm 24: "The earth is the LORD'S, and everything in it, the world, and all who live in it; for he founded it upon the seas and established it upon the waters" (vv. 1-2). Despite the claims of dominion thinkers, the earth is *not* ours, nor did God create it for us to do with as we please. In truth, there is no scriptural basis for arguing that the earth *belongs* to any of its creatures. It is the Creator who holds the earth's title; it is God who is Lord and landlord. The nature of our habitation on earth can be no more than that of favored tenants, a fact that fundamentally alters the meaning of dominion. Anyone who has ever rented a home or apartment is well aware of the limitations of tenancy. Can a renter remodel apart from the owner's permission? Don't renter and landlord need to be in clear communication about any changes to the home? Aren't the wishes and the will of the landlord clearly spelled out in written form? Our occupancy of God's earth is no different!

2. A deeper theology must also take into account what the biblical record says about the character and value given to the creation by the Creator. The final words of Genesis 1 offer a most revealing summation of a claim made throughout the story of creation: "God saw all that he had made, and it was very good" (Genesis 1:31). And even before this final exclamation, "it was good" rings out six times as a litany of affirmation. It is as if God were saying, "Make no doubt about it: all that I have made is good! Every rock, every beating heart, every molecule." If we are looking for a foundation upon which to build a deeper theology or to affirm the intrinsic value of the world, we need look no further. The world God made was (and is) a good world. It was good not because human beings found it useful or amenable to their exploitation. It was good because God made it that way. Creation's worth is no less intrinsic than our own.

This realization should give us pause before we consider any course of action that risks exploiting the environment and defiling the Creator's good work.

3. A third biblical affirmation for a deeper theology comes from the second account of creation, located in Genesis 2. There we read, "The LORD God took the man and put him in the garden of Eden to work it and take care of it" (Genesis 2:15). Some well-intentioned souls have taken this to mean that our proper role is that of earth's gardeners. Such an image is appealing, but we need to be careful with this one. It is presumptuous to assume that humans have either the knowledge or skill, much less the wisdom, to manage the earth. There is ample environmental evidence to demonstrate the folly of such an interpretation.

Nonetheless, this idyllic scene from the garden of Eden hints at an important truth about the appropriate human attitude toward the created order. Is not the best attitude one that is consistent with God's own attitude toward creation? As we become more willing to reflect the divine concern for the well-being of the world, we reveal our deepening understanding of both the Creator and creation. Here, of course, we must rely heavily on the grace of God in Christ to help us. Yet, a deeper theology becomes almost inevitable when we sincerely take to heart the opportunities given us to care for the world with the same loving spirit as God.

4. This leads us to a final biblical affirmation, one that returns us to the first creation story. It is no accident that the Genesis 1 account of creation speaks in the same breath of both our dominion and our creation in the image and likeness of God. As we "image" the Creator's loving concern for the world, we fulfill the noblest aspirations of our dominion. As James Nash has noted, "Love is the essence of the image, and the assignment of Christians is to reflect that love in relationship with all that God loves." The extent to which our loving attitude toward the world mirrors God's own is a decisive measurement of our growing spiritual and theological depth. The more Godlike or Christlike we become toward one another and the creation, the deeper our theology becomes.

And a deeper theology is exactly what we need! The unbelieving world is waiting to hear what Christians have to say about creation and its care. We must know how to respond. We need to be able to articulate what our Scripture says about our earthly home, not just to save ourselves from embarrassment, but because the Creator knows best how to care for his creation. If God has spoken, and he has, his message must be made known. I urge you to study the Word and all it says about creation and its care. In this way, we will be equipped to present the hope of Jesus Christ to a world caught in a deepening environmental crisis.

I close on this note by sharing the words of another preacher from a more distant time and place. More than a century ago, the blind George Matheson, a minister for the Church of Scotland, prayerfully reflected on the relationship between our dominion over other creatures and the image of God we carry in our being. I have read few words more eloquent than these from Matheson's *Searchings in the Silence*. His heartfelt thoughts, properly heard, will inspire a deepening respect for both creation and Creator.

> God never gives dominion to any creature which has not received his image. His image is love. Other things belong to God; but God is love. No creature that has not love will be allowed to have a permanent empire. The Father of mercy will not put the reins of government into a hand that has no heart. Dominion is a very solemn thing; it may oppress, crush, destroy. The Father must have a guarantee for its gentleness. What guarantee can there be but His own image—the possession of a nature tender as the Divine? Ye who torture the beast of the field, have you considered the ground of your authority? Have you pondered why it is that God has given you the dominion? It is because he meant to give you His image ere you began to reign.

> My Father, fill me with love for things beneath me. Forbid that I should be cruel to the beasts of the field.

Give me the tenderness that is born of reverence. Teach me to revere the creation under me. Was not its life a stream from thy life? Is not its life a mystery to me even now?

Give me fellowship with beast and bird. Let me enter into sympathy with their hunger, their thirst, their weariness, their cold, their frequent homelessness. Let me give their wants a place in my prayers. Let me remember them in the struggles of the forest. Let me remember them in the winter's frost and snow. Let me be to them what Thou hast been to me—a protector, a Providence.

Amen.

[This sermon was preached on June 7, 1992, at Park Avenue Baptist Church, El Dorado, Kansas.]

Whoops!

Madeleine L'Engle

One of the joys of leading writers' workshops is hearing the writers' stories. Let me tell you two, written by the same person, a retired Episcopal priest. The first is a new version of the creation story: "As of now, the general opinion in the scientific world is that everything started with what is familiarly known as the Big Bang. After the Big Bang, the voice of God was heard to say, 'Whoops!'"

The other story was a second assignment. Often for a first assignment, I will ask the writer to turn to Scripture, look up a story about a woman in a time of decision and conflict, and write a story about her. The next assignment is often to take the story and hand it to the person sitting on the left hand. That person is to rewrite the story from the point of view of somebody else in the original story. So this was a second assignment from a story written about Hannah, the mother of Samuel. This writer chose four different points of view. He wrote brief monologues from the point of view of Eli, the priest who was given the child, Samuel, to educate; the child Samuel, himself; Elkanah, Samuel's father; and an angel.

The angel says, "Oh, God, please don't send me back to earth again. It's just terrible. What can I do with these people? Please don't make me go back again, please! What? I don't have to go? You mean it? I don't have to go? Oh, thank you, *thank you!* What? What? You mean—*you're going!*"

Even the angel was surprised.

God! God coming to earth! God, caring enough about us recalcitrant creatures to come to us!

It used to be taught that God has no need of us, that God has no needs at all. It also used to be taught that God is our parent. Two contradictory points of view! If children have need of their parents, the parents also have need of the children. My children are grown and out of the nest, and I try not to interfere, but I am still part of their lives, even from a distance. I need to be in touch, by phone, and as often as possible in person. I need to love them. I care what happens to them.

It is my belief that God cares about what happens to creation and about all that happens to every single one of us who has been made. I don't really think God said, "Whoops!" What I believe God said is, "It is good! It is very good!" God said this even after he had made the human beings who betray him over and over again. Judas's betrayal of Jesus is the one we focus on, but it began with Adam and Eve.

There's a story that when God made Adam, God looked at him and said, "I can do better." But did he? It seems to me we all trip over pride, arrogance, and resentment, and fall flat on our faces, regardless of whether we're male or female. And God still cares about us, loves us enough to come to us, as one of us. God is here, with us, part of the story, all through the Hebrew Scriptures. In ancient thinking, an angel was not only an aspect of God, an angel *was* God. When Abraham was speaking with the angel about the fate of Sodom and Gomorrah, suddenly he was speaking to God *'el*self: "Will not the Judge of all the earth do right?" (Genesis 18:25). Bold talk, wasn't it? But Abraham had learned to be secure in God's love.

Today it seems that there is a great deal of insecurity about God's love, and a great fear of God's anger. Surely we give God cause for anger, but I think again of my husband and myself as human parents. Sure, occasionally we get mad at our children, but as Jesus said, "Which of you fathers, if your son asks for a fish, will give him a snake instead? Or if he asks for an egg, will give him a scorpion?" (Luke 11:11-12). And Jesus goes on to point out that he is talking about human parents! How much greater is the Father's love for us!

We human parents love our children as best as we can, and though it's often not enough, far more often we are grieved rather than angered when they do something they should not have done. I suspect we grieve God more often than we anger him: "My children, my children, how could you have done this? How can you behave this way?"

When Adam and Eve listened to the tempter rather than to God, God came after them in the cool of the evening, calling for them: "Where are you?" (Genesis 3:9). "Where are you," God asks of us when we turn away. "Where are you?"

Sometimes we reply. "I'm here. What is it?" And often we are reluctant. Isaiah said, "I am a man of unclean lips" (Isaiah 6:5). Jeremiah said, "I am only a child" (Jeremiah 1:6). Moses stuttered and tried to get out of doing what God asked of him. Gideon said, "You can't mean me!" The only one I can think of offhand who said yes immediately was Mary: When the angel came to her with his incredible demand, she replied, "Be it unto me according to thy word" (Luke 1:38 KJV). Mary had total faith in God and in God's word, and faith that God's word was love. Could anyone who did not believe completely in God's love have given birth to All Love, the God who came to us as Jesus?

God almost always asks the impossible. If it is possible, if it is easy, we can almost always be sure that it is the tempter asking, not God. God asked Abraham to leave his comfortable home, long after retirement age; to go to a strange land with his wife, who was long past childbearing years; and to start a family. God asked Gideon to free his captured people from a vast enemy, far more powerful than the little groups of Jews hiding in the mountains. God asked the prophets not to foretell the future but to tell the people where they were, right then, where they had gone wrong, where they had stopped listening to the God of love—that they had become, as a whole, far more secular than we are in our secular cities today. And he asked Mary to give birth to Jesus, who was going to save us from ourselves and from our sins.

And Jesus? What did God ask of Jesus, and who was Jesus? Jesus was God, for starters. If our Christianity is trinitarian, we believe that Christ, the second person of the Trinity, left the

Godhead to come to us as a human being, to live with us, to show us what it is to be human. If we are trinitarian Christians, we are asked to believe that Jesus was totally human and totally divine. That, of course, is impossible.

Yes, once again, God asks of us the impossible. We can be reluctant. Throughout history, most of God's chosen people have been reluctant. We can say, "It's impossible!" and turn away. We can, as some Christians have done, emphasize the deity of Jesus to the exclusion of his humanity, and we can, as other Christians have done, emphasize his humanity at the expense of his divinity. It's lots easier. But God doesn't ask easy things. Satan does. When Satan tempted Jesus after his baptism, all the temptations were for Jesus to take the easy way out. And Jesus, being fully human and fully divine, refused Satan's wiles. God does ask the impossible. And with God's help, we can say, with Mary, "Be it unto me according to thy word."

When I am in a quandary about something, I usually ask, "What would Jesus do?" And often I don't know the answer. Life at the end of the twentieth century is very different from life two thousand years ago. But I know that whatever Jesus' answer would be, it would be the loving answer. And love, like Jesus, is seldom easy. When it's easy, it's sentimentality, not love. Love often says no when we would like the answer to be yes. Jesus did not allow all the people whom he had cured to follow him as one of his disciples. He told them to stay where they were and to spread the word of love, and often they were disbelieved. He didn't let the rich young man—keeping all his riches—come to him. Whenever Jesus calls us, something has to be given away: our self-will, our eagerness to make judgments about other people's sins. Whenever I judge another, I can almost hear Jesus telling me to look at my own sins instead.

We live in a judgmental era, particularly in the church. We point fingers at other people's sins. Some, indeed, have sinned. But what about mercy? Several years ago I spoke at an Assemblies of God college in the Midwest, and during the question-and-answer session, one young man stood up and said, "Your books really do indicate that you believe that God is forgiving."

"What an extraordinary statement," I replied.

"No, no," he corrected himself. "What I really mean is that your books seem to indicate that ultimately God is going to forgive everybody."

I give my best answers when I don't have time to think and get in the way. I heard myself saying, "I don't think God is going to fail with creation. I don't believe in a failing God. Do you want God to fail?"

"But there has to be absolute justice," the young man said.

"Is that what you want?" I asked. "Absolute justice? You're maybe nineteen or twenty. If you should die tonight, wouldn't you want at least a tiny little bit of mercy? Me, I want lots and lots of mercy. Don't you feel the need of any mercy at all?"

But that had not occurred to him.

And mercy, like love, is not easy. As one of the characters in my new novel says firmly, "Mercy and permissiveness are not the same thing." God's love is totally free, and if we accept this gift, God's love is also totally demanding.

So do I understand the Incarnation? Of course not. I live by it, but it is far beyond my finite, human comprehension. Scripture tells me that it is God loving us so much that he sends his beloved Son to us for our salvation. It is an ultimate act of love on the part of the infinite God. It is when we insist on understanding the Infinite that we get into trouble, trouble that caused the Crusaders to slaughter Greek Christians; that a few centuries later caused the Inquisition, Christians burning Christians; and that a few centuries later caused Catholics and Puritans to murder and destroy each other because each group thought that they had *the* truth and that the other group was absolutely wrong. It is when we insist on defining God's love or God's anger that we blunder into anti-Semitism or join rigid sects that promise us all the answers.

God does not give answers; God gave himself to save us and to free us from our sins. Jesus was born in a barn in Bethlehem. That tiny baby, robed in created human flesh, went on to bear the sins of our flesh on the cross. How heavy his burden must have been during his last weeks on earth when he knew that his dearest friends did not understand him and were going to betray him. How heavy our sins must have been when he hung on the cross. But for love of us, he carried them. How blessed we are in this love!

Why can't we remember his last commandment, that we should love each other as he loved us? John, in his epistle, tells us firmly that if we cannot love each other, love the people we know, we cannot love God! If we are able truly to love one another, then we will get a glimpse of understanding of the magnificent love of God.

This Is My Father's World

Bishop George D. McKinney Jr.

The earth is the LORD'S, and everything in it,
   the world, and all who live in it;
for he founded it upon the seas
   and established it upon the waters.
            —Psalm 24:1-2

The LORD God took the man and put him in the Garden of
Eden to work it and take care of it.
            Genesis 2:15

The familiar hymn by Maltbie Babcock, "This Is My Father's
World," sets to music the profound truth of Psalm 24:1-2. This
text, which declares God's ownership of the earth and all creation, is a solid foundation for "a theology of environmental
protection and preservation." This text refutes the argument that
the earth and its riches belong to the powerful who take and hold
them—or to the masses who struggle to obtain the same riches,
and who sometimes squander them. No! The creation of our
Lord does not belong to the *rich* who possess it nor to the *poor*
who need and want the resources. Neither the greedy nor the
needy can claim ownership! God owns everything! The earth is
the Lord's! It is the Lord's by "divine right." He created it. "For
he founded it upon the seas and established it upon the waters."

In Genesis 2, God, the Creator and Owner of earth and the
universe, has provided a lush garden that is environmentally
perfect. The vegetation was watered by a "mist" that went up
from "the earth." The fruit trees and the "ornamental" trees,
which were pleasant to the sight, were watered by a great river

with four tributaries. This rich garden of Eden with its vegetation, animals, and minerals—including gold, onyx, and bdellium—was prepared by God to be the first home of men and women. Adam and Eve are placed in this idyllic reserve with specific instructions to "work it and take care of it" (Genesis 2:15). God's instructions are clear: "Adam, you are to preserve and protect your environment." With this action, God made humans the stewards or overseers in charge of protecting and preserving God's property. God's directions for the environmental protection of Eden are the same directions for the protection of any locale that humankind may call home—Africa, Asia, Europe, the Americas, and everywhere that people live. Human responsibility and accountability to God are neither altered nor canceled by a person's religion or irreligion, politics, race, social status, or any other condition. To deny this responsibility is an act of rebellion against God; to destroy creation wantonly is to *sin* against God, against our neighbors, and against the generations that follow us.

It is indeed one of the great tragedies of our era that the church, the community of faith, has not maintained a proper focus on developing a biblical theology of environmental protection and preservation. Too often our theologians, pastors, and laity have been silent as our rivers and streams are polluted by industrial wastes; as our air becomes contaminated by poisons that threaten life; as the ozone layer is pierced, exposing human life to deadly radiation; and as the food supply is contaminated and the environmental balance is upset by the destruction of the rain forest, trees, and vegetation.

The community of faith cannot be silent any longer. We must speak out and proclaim that *all* unrighteousness is sin. It is unrighteous to denude the forest, to pollute the air, and to squander the richness of the earth. Creation does *not* belong to humans; it is God's property. Therefore, to disrespect God's authority and ownership is to commit both the sin of disobedience and the sin of rebellion. This egregious sin against our environment must not only become a part of our discussion of the doctrine of sin in sermons and textbooks; it must become a part of our confession and repentance. The community of faith, the church, at the close of the century must reexamine and redefine its categories of sin to include sin against the environment, along with the sins of racism, sexism, classism, and materialism.

Sin

A biblical theology of environmental protection dispels the myth of unlimited resources. While God created animals and plants to bear seed to multiply and replenish the earth, this replacement process involves tending, keeping, preserving, and protecting by human beings. Our failure to preserve and protect has resulted in the poisoning of fish in our rivers, streams, and oceans; in the slaughtering of animals, not for food but for fun and games; and in the strip mining of minerals and the destruction of trees and forests for greed and profit. Now the results of the sins of our fathers and our own sins are more than we can bear. In our cities, the air we breathe is unhealthy; our food supply is contaminated, resulting in untold deaths from cancer and other diseases; and many animal species are endangered or extinct. Yes, the wages of *sin*—including sin against the environment—is death: the death of vegetation and animals, the death of humanity, physically and spiritually.

When God gave us our home in Eden, there was an abundance of fresh air, fresh food, and fresh water. The continual supply of the necessities of life was contingent on faithful stewardship, "working and caring for" the garden. The failure of humans resulted in the destruction of the ecological balance, the proliferation of disease, and early death for humans and animals.

I can never forget the sight of emaciated, starving, dying children and adults caused by human abuse of the land and rape of the environment. Nor can I ever forget the sight of millions of dead fish floating downstream through the heart of a major American city. As a resident of southern California, I know the discomfort and fear of trying to breathe and survive during the frequent smog alerts. In many American communities, the water supply is so contaminated that it must be sterilized before drinking or household use.

Here is a word from the Lord to us today—"And you may be sure that your sin will find you out" (Numbers 32:23). We have lost our fresh air, fresh food, and fresh water. Yet all is not hopeless. Our God is a God of mercy, forgiveness, and restoration: "If my people, who are called by my name, will humble themselves and pray and seek my face and turn from their wicked ways, then will I hear from heaven and will forgive their sin and will heal their land" (2 Chronicles 7:14).

Healing

The prerequisite for the healing of our land—spiritually, socially, environmentally—includes two steps. First, we must agree with God that we have sinned against him, against ourselves, and against future generations. By our disobedience and rebellion, we have failed to acknowledge God as the owner of everything; we have *neglected* our responsibility to tend and keep our environment and resources; and we have *failed* to be accountable stewards.

Second, the healing of the land requires repentance, that is, a change in direction, a radical reversal from the old, selfish, profit-seeking, materialistic world-view. The earth is the Lord's and everything in it—the earth, all of creation, the whole universe—is *holy*.

> Earth is crammed with Heaven.
> And every bush aflame with God.
> But only those who see take off their shoes.
> —Elizabeth Barrett Browning

Everything belongs to God, and what is holy must not be profaned or secularized by abuse, neglect, or misuse.

This required change of direction will involve a return to respect for the sabbath concept. We must revisit the laws governing the sabbath rest for people, animals, and the land. Rest allows people, animals, and the Lord's land to experience renewal and restoration.

Jesus affirms that the sabbath was made for people (see Mark 3:1-6). Observance of the sabbath saves us from ceaseless activity and perpetual motion. It teaches us that God is in charge and running things, whether we are awake or sleep, working or resting. For it is God who works in us to will and to do what pleases him.

Justice

Finally, a biblical theology of environmental preservation and protection must include an expanded concept of justice. In traditional Christian theology, justice is viewed as a vertical relationship between God and people. It is God's fair and equitable dealing with humankind, which is guided by his truth, holiness, and love.

Here are a few texts that show God's justice for all people: "He causes his sun to rise on the evil and the good, and sends rain on the righteous and the unrighteous" (Matthew 5:45); "For every living soul belongs to me, the father as well as the son—both alike belong to me. The soul who sins is the one who will die" (Ezekiel 18:4); "If we confess our sins, he is faithful and just and will forgive us our sins and purify us from all unrighteousness" (1 John 1:9).

On the other hand, horizontal justice—that is, justice in human relationships—derives from our relationship with God, who demanded that we practice love and forgiveness in response to his grace. God, who made us and redeemed us through Jesus Christ, requires that we love one another. Justice prevails in human relationships when we practice love. Love for God, self, and others fulfills the law and the prophets. In this light, doing justice is living under God's authority in loving obedience: "He has showed you, O man, what is good. And what does the LORD require of you? To act justly and to love mercy and to walk humbly with your God" (Micah 6:8).

Yet there is a third dimension to justice. This third dimension concerns humans and their relationship to creation. The same God who commanded us to love one another also commands us to work and take care of the garden. Here, humans find that God has delegated to them authority and responsibility to protect and preserve what we do not own, what belongs to God. God did not abdicate ownership. Rather, God appointed a steward, a caretaker. Justice demands that the steward faithfully execute the assigned responsibility.

May we remember that we are accountable first to God, then to ourselves and to future generations. Our environment, our home, was once a "garden" with a wealth of good things and an abundance of blessings—fresh air, fresh food, and fresh water. There was balance and beauty that reflected the genius of the Creator. Greed, injustice, and sin against God have corrupted our environment. Here is our hope. He who created in the beginning can re-create today in response to our faith and repentance. It is my prayer and hope that our repentance will bring healing to our poisoned planet and troubled land.

> This is my Father's world,
> And to my listening ears
> All nature sings,
> And round me rings
> The music of the spheres.
> This is my Father's world:
> O let me ne'er forget
> That though the wrong
> Seems oft so strong,
> God is the Ruler yet.
>   —Maltbie D. Babcock, 1901

The Balanced Life

Earl F. Palmer

This Sunday, we come to the fifth sermon in a series on the Ten Commandments. Today, we want to look at the Fourth Commandment. The Ten Commandments are recorded for us in two places in the Old Testament, Exodus 20 and Deuteronomy 5, but the two texts provide different versions of this commandment.

> Remember the Sabbath day by keeping it holy. Six days you shall labor and do all your work, but the seventh day is a Sabbath to the LORD your God. On it you shall not do any work, neither you, nor your son or daughter, nor your manservant or maidservant, nor your animals, nor the alien within your gates. For in six days the LORD made the heavens and the earth, the sea, and all that is in them, but he rested on the seventh day. Therefore the LORD blessed the Sabbath day and made it holy.
>
> —Exodus 20:8-11

In Deuteronomy 5, we read a longer presentation of the Fourth Commandment. Please note the word *sabbath* in the text. It is a word that does double duty in the Old Testament. A significant word, it is used about seventy-five times. *Sabbath* has a variety of important meanings—"cease," "rest," "week," "seven," and "sabbath day of rest." All these meanings appear in these two versions of the Fourth Commandment.

> Observe the Sabbath day by keeping it holy, as the LORD your God has commanded you. Six days you shall labor and do all your work, but the seventh day is a

Sabbath to the LORD your God. On it you shall not do
any work, neither you, nor your son or daughter, nor
your manservant or maidservant, nor your ox, your
donkey or any of your animals, nor the alien within your
gates, so that your manservant and maidservant may
rest, as you do. [*Now, here's the part that is different
from Exodus. In Exodus, we are also told to "remember" the goodness of creation. In Deuteronomy, we are
to "remember" God's redemption. So we have these two
great memories that we are to have on the sabbath day.*]
Remember that you were slaves in Egypt and that the
LORD your God brought you out of there with a mighty
hand and an outstretched arm. Therefore the LORD your
God has commanded you to observe the Sabbath day.
                                    —Deuteronomy 5:12-15

This is the Fourth Commandment. What does it mean for us?
In New Testament times, this commandment was often the
center of stormy controversies. The people of the first century
focused on this commandment more than any of the others.
What was its power? What does the Fourth Commandment say?
Let's look at the many things it teaches us about ourselves, about
the earth, and about God's will for the earth.

Humans

The Fourth Commandment says our lives are organized into
a seven-day cycle. The number seven is important in the Old
Testament and often symbolizes fulfillment and completion. In
this commandment, the seven-day cycle sets boundaries for our
lives and helps us understand the way we are to live: six days
of labor and one day of rest. There is a rhythm built into our
lives. Notice also that we are mandated both to work and to rest
within those seven days.

The Fourth Commandment also calls us to be "rememberers"
during those seven days. What an interesting perspective God
has on humans—we are to be "rememberers." In Exodus, we

are to remember the creation of the earth, and in Deuteronomy, we are to remember that God redeems us.

Notice too that the scope of the Fourth Commandment extends beyond humans; it has to do with animals, the earth, and even foreigners. This focus on the foreigner or alien sets the Jewish law apart from the laws of other ancient Near Eastern societies. Only Jewish law was concerned with protecting foreigners. The Jews were to practice equal justice, which spreads beyond race or clan.

This commandment is obviously very positive. Some commandments are negative, but the Fourth Commandment uses positive words and concepts. The description of life as a rhythmic balance is quite positive, and we will benefit if we obey its terms.

Let's think now about the themes of "rest" and "work" in this commandment. Our cycle of seven days is divided into periods of rest and work.

Rest

According to the Fourth Commandment, we are the creatures who need to stop, to cease, to think, to worship, and to remember. We are the creatures who need time to collect our thoughts, and we function best when we have a rhythmic balance of work and rest within each week.

By the way, in Exodus 23, the sabbath law is expanded to include the land. The land can be worked for six years, but in the seventh year, it is to lie fallow, which means it is to rest. Land banks did not originate with the New Deal and the United States Department of Agriculture! Land banks are an ecological concept related to humans' rhythmic relationship with the earth. Here in the Fourth Commandment, we have the beginnings of a doctrine of ecology. You can see what a *vital* commandment this is when it is rightly understood.

But Exodus 23 also reveals an ethical component to the Fourth Commandment. "Let the land lie unplowed and unused. Then the poor among your people may get food from it, and the wild animals may eat what they leave. Do the same with your vineyard and your olive grove" (Exodus 23:11). There is to be a balance among the earth, the poor, and the animals. There is an ethical obligation not to overharvest the land for ourselves but to let it rest so that other creatures, both human and nonhuman, can enjoy it as well. The law gives us a balanced view of how to live on the earth. The earth needs rest, too.

By the way, I read a fascinating article that described how zoos are learning that their animals become fatigued and stressed if they are gawked at seven days a week. Zoos are beginning to realize that even animals need a rest. So some zoos are instituting a day off for the animals, so that they might have a little privacy!

The law signals a need that we have to function within a rhythm of work and rest. The law pays us a compliment. We are not machines that can endlessly grind on. We need balance.

Work

Ah! Work is a part of the rhythm, too. There is no easy way to work. Perhaps in ancient Israel work was even harder than it is today. We are to rest one day and work six days.

I've heard it said, "Sweat is one thing money cannot buy." Think about this for a moment. You can join all the health clubs you want. You can pay your dues, but you will not sweat. You may sweat out of anxiety over how to pay those dues. But the sweat that comes from labor is something that money cannot buy. You have to work; I have to work. There is no easy way to get around this.

A few years ago, I spoke at a conference in Canada. One of the participants was a horse wrangler, and he was dressed to fit the part—blue jeans, cowboy boots, cowboy hat. I didn't know very much about horses, so I struck up a conversation with this young man. I asked him to tell me about horses. I was particularly interested in how horses handle the Canadian winters. As a Californian, I knew nothing about winter! I asked if they ride the horses in winter and was told that the horses enjoy the exercise in the middle of winter, even with temperatures of forty degrees below zero. Then this wrangler told me that the downside of riding in the winter is that the horses must be towel dried after the trip because they sweat. Being sweaty in the frigid Canadian air is not a good idea for humans, and it is not a good idea for horses. Both are liable to get sick. So precautions must be taken to dry the horses, which takes about thirty minutes. That's thirty minutes for a wrangler to stand around in the bitter cold drying a horse, and then the next horse wants to go for a ride and needs to be towel dried. In that moment, I realized that there is no easy way to be a wrangler! It's hard work. I think of all the horse movies I saw as a child: Gene Autrey, Roy Rogers, Trigger. Those are pretty sentimental portrayals of life on the ranch!

There is *no easy way* to work. And yet Scripture says we are supposed to work. Work is a part of the rhythm of life. Resting and remembering is a part of life, but so is working and doing things with my hands and body. Young people need to feel good about their heart *and* hands, their head *and* feet. Rest and work.

Three Principles

Let's look at three truths from this commandment.

1. *The Fourth Commandment is a "freedom commandment" and a "dominion commandment."* The doctrine of freedom in the Old Testament begins in the garden of Eden when Adam and Eve were given the responsibility to have dominion over the earth. This *does not* mean humans have the right to exploit the earth; it means humans have the duty of tending the earth. It means humans are called to work toward ecological balance in the earth.

The freedom that God gave us can be seen in our privilege to name the animals. This was our first "freedom act." The animals don't name us (as far as we know!), but we name them. We pick out a name, sometimes an outlandish one, like *hippopotamus.* Then the poor hippopotamus is stuck with that name for the rest of its life! And God even calls the animals by the name that we give them. He allows us to do this. It is a role that we get to play. The privilege of naming is powerful; it is about dominion.

The Fourth Commandment is related to dominion in that we are given the power and the freedom to find our work and to find our rest. God does *not* say, "You shall be available for work on Mondays, and you shall be available for rest on the sabbath." The command says, "*You* find your work and *you* find your rest." Each one is held responsible to work and to rest in each week. Be proactive: find your own work, find something to do. You are likewise responsible for your own rest. This is a part of your dominion. This freedom to be proactive is actually a compliment to our dignity.

2. *The Fourth Commandment carries no time limits.* Notice what this commandment does *not* say—"For six days you shall work, up until the golden age of sixty-five, when your company puts you to pasture with a golden wrist watch, and *then* you can rest for the remainder of your life." That doctrine of retirement is an evil doctrine. I want to call the bluff on what could be called "retirement theology." It is bad theology. This is like putting a person on the shelf and saying, "We don't need you anymore." The Bible does not have a doctrine of retirement, but it does have a doctrine of discipleship. Six days you shall labor and one day you shall rest, *until the day you die.* Here is an example of the death of a successful person: "I'm sorry; Sarah cannot come to her Bible class today; she just died." Or, "Sarah can't come to her saxophone lesson today; she just died." Why? Sarah lived with dignity right up until the day she died, maintaining that rhythm of work and rest. (Sometimes we may need the assistance of a hospital or a rest home, but generally a biblical pattern of life has us active right up until our death.)

3. *The Fourth Commandment builds balance into our lives.* Do you know what causes burnout? We push ourselves in our work and put too many expectations on a vacation that is far too short. We ask too much of our vacations, and they cannot provide what we need. The biblical plan contains rest within *each* seven-day period. Everything must have balance: time with family, time with friends; reading for our work, reading

things for pleasure. You will not burn out if you have a rhythm within each seven-day period. You must have seven days that make sense.

Conclusion

Saint Augustine said, "Our hearts are restless until they rest in Thee. God who is ever at work and ever at rest, may we be ever at work and ever at rest." Is your life balanced? God wants it to be.

Let us pray: Heavenly Father, thank you for this commandment. It is a good commandment. It will bring goodness and blessing to those who order their lives by its wisdom. Lord, I pray for each of us that we will be able to make sense out of each week in our lives. Help us to be proactive with the time you have given to us. Help us to live balanced lives. In Christ's name we pray. Amen.

[This sermon was preached on February 7, 1993, at University Presbyterian Church in Seattle, Washington.]

Tending the Garden without Worshiping It

Ron Sider

You and I have a problem—in fact three problems. The environmental crisis is not a silly fiction created by mad scientists and political demagogues. There are dangerous holes in the ozone layer. Our waters, soil, and air are polluted. Spreading carbon dioxide emissions from our cars and factories threaten to cause global warming that could raise ocean levels, flooding vast land areas and destroying some of our great coastal cities. In the last forty years, we have lost one-third of our rain forests. In the last forty years, we also have lost one-fifth of all the world's topsoil. We don't have to be very good mathematicians to figure out that if we keep losing resources at this rate for a couple more forty-year periods, we will be in terrible trouble. There *is* an environmental crisis.

But we also have a second problem. Some of the people most concerned about the ecological dangers tell us that historic Christianity is the problem. We must, they tell us, reject the biblical teaching that the Creator is distinct from the earth and that people alone are made in the image of God. Actress Shirley MacLaine tells us that we must become Eastern monists and believe that you and I are gods. Others tell us to worship the goddess, Mother Earth. Catholic theologian Matthew Fox tells us that we should turn away from a theology that talks a great deal about sin, grace, and redemption, and develop instead a "creation spirituality," with nature, rather than the Bible, as our primary revelation and sin a distant memory. And Australian scientist Peter Singer says that people are no more important than monkeys and mosquitoes. To think that we are more important is "speciesism."

Fortunately, biblical Christians reject this theological nonsense. But then so often we turn around and worship the earth in a different way. By the cars we drive, the houses we purchase, the affluent lifestyles we live, we show that we really worship the god of materialistic consumerism. That's our third problem.

I hope and pray that Christians plunge deeply into the environmental struggle to preserve a decent earth for our grandchildren. But for God's sake, let's not become environmentalists because that is trendy and politically correct and the currently fashionable liberation movement. Not every so-called liberation movement is biblical. Some represent a clear rejection of the way God wants us to live.

Christians must become vigorous environmentalists because God's Word demands it, because we are destroying the Creator's garden, and because many secular environmentalists are on a deep spiritual pilgrimage. If we don't show them that biblical faith is what they are looking for, they will find some other religious foundation for their ecological concerns.

Make no mistake: a spiritual battle is raging; Satan would love nothing better than to persuade modern people that the best way to solve our environmental crisis is to abandon historic Christian truth. The way to defeat Satan is for all Christians to become committed environmentalists and to ground their struggle to save the earth on solid biblical foundations. To do that, four biblical principles are especially crucial.

First, we must hold together God's transcendence and God's immanence. God is different from—*God transcends*—creation. But God is also *in* creation. If we focus only on God's immanence (his presence in the world), we land in pantheism, where everything is divine and good as it is. If we talk only about God's transcendence (his radical separateness from creation), we may end up seeing nature as a mere tool to be used at human whim.

The biblical God is both immanent and transcendent. God is not a cosmic watchmaker who wound up the global clock and now lets it run on its own. God continues to work in creation. In

Job we read that God gives orders to the morning (38:12), that the eagle soars at God's commands (39:27), and that God provides food for the ravens when their young cry out in hunger (38:41). The Creator, however, is also radically distinct from the creation. Creation is finite, limited, dependent; the Creator is infinite, unlimited, self-sufficient.

Second, human beings are both interdependent with the rest of creation, and unique within it. Sometimes we Christians have forgotten our interdependence with the rest of creation. Our daily existence depends on water, sun, and air. Everything is interrelated in the global ecosystem. The emissions from our cars contribute to the destruction of trees—trees that convert the carbon dioxide we breathe out into the oxygen we need to breathe in. Christians today must recover an appreciation of our dependence on the trees and flowers, the streams and forests. Unless we do, we shall surely perish.

But the Bible insists on two other things about humanity: human beings *alone* are created in the image of God, and we *alone* have been given a special "dominion" or stewardship. It is a biblical truth, not speciesism, to say that only human beings—and not trees and animals—are created in the image of God (Genesis 1:27). This truth is the foundation of our God-given mandate to be stewards over the nonhuman creation (Genesis 1:28; Psalm 8).

If our status is no different from that of animals and plants, we cannot eat them for food or use them to build civilizations. We do *not* need to apologize to Brother Carrot when we have lunch. We are free to use the resources of the earth for human purposes. Created in the divine image, we alone have been placed in charge of the earth. At the same time, our dominion must be the gentle care of a loving gardener, not the callous exploitation of a self-centered lord. So we should not wipe out species or waste the nonhuman creation. Only a careful, stewardly use of plants and animals by human beings is legitimate.

Tragically, and arrogantly, we have distorted "dominion" into "domination." Lynn White was correct in placing some blame for environmental decay on Christianity. A *misunderstanding* of the Bible, and not God's Word itself, is at fault here.

Genesis 2:15 says the Lord put us in the garden "to work it and take care of it." The word translated "work" is the Hebrew word *'abad,* and it means "to serve." The related noun actually means "slave" or "servant." The word translated "take care of" is the Hebrew word *shamar,* which suggests watchful care and preservation of the earth. We are to serve and watch lovingly over God's good garden, not rape it.

The second biblical principle, then, is that human beings do have a unique status in creation, but we are also interdependent with the rest of creation.

Third, we need a God-centered, rather than a human-centered, world-view. This is important if we are to respect the independent worth of the nonhuman creation. Christians have easily and too often fallen into the trap of supposing that the nonhuman creation has worth only as it serves human purposes. This, however, is not a biblical perspective.

Genesis 1 makes clear that all creation is good—good, according to the story, even before our first ancestors arrived on the scene. Colossians 1:16 reveals that all things are created for *Christ.* The text doesn't say they are created for you and me, although that's part of the truth. Here it says the creation was made *for Christ!* And according to Job 39:1-2, God watches over the doe in the mountains. She may never see a human being, but God counts the months of her pregnancy and watches over her when she gives birth! The first purpose of the nonhuman creation, then, is to glorify God, not to serve us.

And creation is part of God's revelation to us:

The heavens are telling the glory of God;
    and the firmament proclaims his handiwork.
Day to day pours forth speech,
    and night to night declares knowledge.
There is no speech, nor are there words;
    their voice is not heard;
yet their voice goes out through all the earth,

and their words to the end of the world.
—Psalm 19:1-4 (RSV)

It is important to note that God has a covenant, not only with people, but also with the nonhuman creation. Did you realize that after the Flood, God made a covenant with the *animals,* as well as with Noah? Listen to Genesis 9:9-10 (RSV): "Behold, I establish my covenant with you and your descendants after you, *and* with every living creature that is with you, the birds, the cattle, and every beast of the earth with you, as many as came out of the ark."

Jesus recognized God's covenant with the whole of creation when he noted how God feeds the birds and clothes the lilies (Matthew 6:26-30). The nonhuman creation has its own worth and dignity apart from its service to humanity.

Insisting on the independent dignity of the nonhuman creation does not mean that we ignore the biblical teaching that it has been given to us human beings for our stewardship and use. But always our use of the nonhuman creation must be a thoughtful stewardship that honors the creation's independent dignity and worth in the eyes of the Creator.

Finally, God's cosmic plan of redemption includes the nonhuman creation. This fact provides a crucial foundation for building a Christian theology for an environmental age. Romans 8 shows that the whole created order, including the material world of bodies and rivers and trees, will be part of the heavenly kingdom. That truth confirms that the created order is good and important.

The Bible's affirmation of the material world can be seen most clearly in Christ himself: not only did the Creator enter his creation by becoming flesh and blood to redeem us from our sin, but the God-man was resurrected *bodily* from the tomb. The goodness of the created order is also revealed in how the Bible describes the coming kingdom. In the marriage supper of the Lamb, we will feast on bread, wine, and all the glorious fruit of the earth.

Unlike Eastern monists who think the created order is an

illusion to escape, biblical people know that the creation is in itself *so good* that God is going to purge it of the evil introduced by the Fall and restore it to wholeness. Romans 8 tells us that at Christ's return, when we experience the resurrection of the body, then the groaning creation will be transformed: "The creation itself will be liberated from its bondage to decay and brought into the glorious freedom of the children of God" (Romans 8:21).

Colossians 1 shows that God intends to reconcile all things, "whether things on earth or things in heaven" (v. 16), through Jesus Christ. That does not mean that everyone will be saved. What it does mean is that Christ's salvation will finally extend to all of creation. The Fall's corruption of every part of creation will be corrected.

If you walk out of the Philadelphia Convention Center and turn right, you come to the Schuylkill River. It's badly polluted. You can catch fish there, but you had better not eat them! If you go left, you soon come to the Delaware River. That's also a mess.

In the coming kingdom, I hope to go sailing on unpolluted Delaware and Schuylkill rivers. I'm not sure about fishing in the kingdom. Maybe we won't fish there. But if we won't, then I'm sure there will be something even more wonderful (although as a devoted fisherman, I have trouble imagining what could *be* more wonderful!).

We need a theology both of creation and of redemption. The Christian hope for Christ's return must be joined with our doctrine of creation. Knowing that we are summoned by the Creator to be wise gardeners who care for God's good earth, knowing the hope that someday the earth will be restored, Christians should be vigorous participants in the environmental movement.

Obviously, God's word compels us to become more concerned with our environment, so that means we must change. That means *more* than recycling bottles or newspapers, however, although that is a good place to start. We need to repent of our unspoken belief that more is better, that more and more material abundance brings fulfillment. We must consume less and switch to renewable resources. The list of concrete things you and I can do goes on and on. If you want more help, I invite you to join forces with one of the several new Christian organizations that are leading evangelicals in caring for creation. We can avoid ecological disaster if we are willing to change.

Precisely as we think about what to do to save the earth, one thing is very striking. Many of the things we need to do for creation are identical with our responsibility to feed the hungry and empower the poor. Thirty-five thousand people have died today of starvation. One-quarter of the world's people live near absolute poverty. For a couple of decades now, Christians have been hearing the message that we must live more simply so that others may simply live. We know that we should reduce our affluent lifestyles, so we can share more with others who are hungry or who need a small loan to earn a decent living.

To be honest with you, I don't know how to plead with Christians forcefully enough to reject today's affluent materialism. We have Jesus' warning that if we don't feed the hungry, we go to hell. We pastors and teachers have the biblical warning that if we fail to say as much about God's concern for the poor as the Bible does, we are heretical, timid shepherds, responsible for our people's materialism. We could do so much more. And I fear that we are losing the battle. Is it not true that most Christians today are more trapped in a practical materialism that treasures *things* more than *Jesus?* Were previous generations of Christians as captivated by materialism as we are now? It would be especially hypocritical if we condemned New Age environmentalists for their worship of the earth and then continued rushing madly down our present path of ever increasing, idolatrous consumerism!

I wish I knew how to help us change directions. Maybe sometimes our call for living more simply has been misunderstood as an ascetic denial of the goodness of the earth, as a call to live in poverty. That's not what I mean.

There is a powerful, wonderful materialism in the Bible. It is different from materialistic consumerism, different from Marxist philosophical materialism, and different from worship of the earth. But it's certainly a kind of materialism.

According to the Bible, as we have seen, the material world is so good that the one who created all things and pronounced them very good actually became flesh. The material world is so good that Jesus rose *bodily* from the tomb. The material world is so good that all believers will be resurrected bodily to dance and revel in a renewed creation when the Lord returns. That's how good the material world is. Consequently, God wants you and me to rejoice now in the good earth's bounty—including wonderful Pennsylvania Dutch cooking.

But there's another side to the biblical teaching. Nothing in the world, not even the whole world, is worth as much as our soul, as our relationship with Jesus Christ. The one who loved to bless wedding feasts calls us to be ready to forsake wife, husband, father, mother, houses, and lands for the sake of his kingdom. Nothing, absolutely nothing, not even everything in the whole world, is as important as a living relationship with Jesus Christ, which leads to life eternal.

I'm afraid that one reason Christians fail to live more simply for the sake of the poor *and* the environment—one reason we persist in our practical materialistic worship of things—is that we don't really love Jesus very much. We substitute lukewarm faith and mere tradition for a passionate love for the Lord and a radical commitment to worship and to obey him at any cost. Colossians 1:18 says Jesus is to "have the supremacy." Is that true for you and me? Is that true for our people?

This Jesus who calls us to save his creation, empower the poor, and work for peace is the Maker of the galaxies, the one in whom all the fullness of God was pleased to dwell. This awesome sovereign will not settle for one-fourth or one-half of our lives. He wants to have first place in everything we think and do.

I don't see much hope for renewing our concern for peace, justice, and the integrity of creation until the Holy Spirit sweeps across our churches, renewing our love for Christ. Person by person, we must turn away from our secret sins, surrender unconditionally to the loving Lord, and invite the Holy Spirit to blow through our lives, empowering us for holiness and self-sacrifice.

In recent weeks, the song "Jesus, You're the Center of My Joy" has frequently been on my mind. It has always moved me deeply, sometimes to tears.

> Jesus, you're the center of my joy.
> All that's good and perfect comes from you.
> You're the heart of my contentment,
> Hope for all I do.
> Jesus, you're the center of my joy.

And I often think of this song along with 2 Corinthians 3:18: "And we, who with unveiled faces all reflect the Lord's glory, are being transformed into his likeness with ever-increasing glory." The veil has been torn away, and we look directly into the awesome face of Christ the Lord, who transforms us.

The church of Jesus Christ will do what God wants it to do for the environment and the poor only if member by member, congregation by congregation, we look up into the face of the risen Lord and submit ourselves totally and unconditionally in worship and obedience. Let's look into his face in surrender as we face every decision—about money, sex, business, marriage, politics, divorce, peacemaking. Can we keep doing some of the things we are now doing if we look constantly and intently into his face and ask him, "My Lord, are you pleased with how I am living, or does it make you weep?" Let's dare daily to look into his face and invite him to make us more and more like himself, transforming us from one degree of glory to another.

I think the church stands at a crossroads. We are educated, sophisticated, socially successful, polished. And some of our churches are dangerously close to being little more than comfortable social clubs, where the successful assemble to renew friendships, traditions, and family connections. The only thing that will save us is a renewal of our love, worship, and obedience to the risen Lord.

I know we face complex decisions and a tumultuous, confusing world. A deeper commitment to Christ will not provide instant, simple solutions. But the central question is as simple as ever. Do I believe that the carpenter from Nazareth, the prophet of peace, the champion of women, the liberator of the poor, is the Creator of the galaxies, the only Savior, the risen Lord, and the returning Redeemer? Will I surrender every nook and cranny of my being to this gentle, loving, awesomely holy Sovereign? Will I worship and obey him with all my heart, soul, and mind?

If he is not the center, the power, and the norm for all we do, then our environmental activity and social concern will be a hollow echo of a well-meaning but often confused world searching desperately, often in the wrong places, for joy, hope, and peace.

So, yes, let's carefully tend the Creator's garden, reveling in its astonishing splendors and awesome glory. But let's worship only the Creator who is also the Redeemer. Let's fall at Jesus' feet in breathless adoration and total surrender, thanking our Beloved for the gorgeous ring he has given us to enjoy, but remembering that the Beloved himself is more precious than all the gems on all the billions of spinning galaxies.

Let's pray.

Lord, in this moment, we stand in your holy presence aware of our sinful failures. With all our hearts we embrace the forgiveness you gladly offer us through your cross. Please change us. Lord, right now we turn our faces to you, we lift our eyes and arms to you, begging you to cleanse our hearts, to take charge of every corner of our being. Make us holy as you are holy. Change us into your likeness. Amen.

Day by day, may it be more and more true for every person here tonight and every person in our congregations:

> Jesus, you're the center of our joy.
> All that's good and perfect comes from you.

You're the heart of our contentment,
Hope for all we do.
Jesus, you're the center of our joy.

[This sermon was delivered to the Mennonite Church General Assembly meeting in Philadelphia, Pennsylvania, on July 31, 1993.]

This World Is Not My Home?

Howard A. Snyder

I consider that our present sufferings are not worth comparing with the glory that will be revealed in us. The creation waits in eager expectation for the sons of God to be revealed. For the creation was subjected to frustration, not by its own choice, but by the will of the one who subjected it, in hope that the creation itself will be liberated from its bondage to decay and brought into the glorious freedom of the children of God. We know that the whole creation has been groaning as in the pains of childbirth right up to the present time. Not only so, but we ourselves, who have the firstfruits of the Spirit, groan inwardly as we wait eagerly for our adoption as sons, the redemption of our bodies. For in this hope we were saved. But hope that is seen is no hope at all. Who hopes for what he already has? But if we hope for what we do not yet have, we wait for it patiently. In the same way, the Spirit helps us in our weakness. We do not know what we ought to pray for, but the Spirit himself intercedes for us with groans that words cannot express. And he who searches our hearts knows the mind of the Spirit, because the Spirit intercedes for the saints in accordance with God's will.

—Romans 8:18-27

Background Texts: Genesis 1:1-13, 31; Psalm 19; Psalm 24
Central Text: The creation itself will be liberated from its bondage to decay and brought into the glorious freedom of the children of God (Romans 8:21).

"This world is not my home; I'm just a-passing through. My treasures are laid up somewhere beyond the blue. . . ."

This is one of the five or so songs I can play on my guitar. Sometimes I play and sing it. But I'm always a little troubled by it. The chorus ends, "and I can't feel at home in this world anymore."

Actually, I feel quite at home in this world. Yes, I know "there's a better world a-coming," and I look forward to that. I know, as Paul says in Philippians 3:20, that "our citizenship is in heaven." But our home, for now, is on the earth.

Having a home in heaven doesn't mean we shouldn't have a home on earth—or *be* at home on earth. Actually, I like the way the Free Methodist English scholar Mary Alice Tenney put it in the title of her book about the Methodist revival in England: *We Are Living in Two Worlds.*

Is this world our home, if we are Christians? In what sense? I want to answer that question by looking at the biblical evidence. What does the Bible say about the earth and about our relationship to it as Christians?

Romans 8 talks about the earth—or, more broadly, about the whole creation. Note especially verses 19-22:

> The creation waits in eager expectation for the sons of God to be revealed. For the creation was subjected to frustration, not by its own choice, but by the will of the one who subjected it, in hope that the creation itself will be liberated from its bondage to decay and brought into the glorious freedom of the children of God. We know that the whole creation has been groaning as in the pains of childbirth right up to the present time.

This is what Romans teaches. But it is part of a broader biblical picture. If we pull together the whole range of biblical teaching—Old Testament and New—we find that there are four great truths about this earth that God has made. I simply want to emphasize these four great truths as we look at this important question: Is this earth our home?

Some of these truths may seem obvious at first glance. But I think we often forget them. We often *talk* and *act* as if the earth were of little concern to God—as if it were merely property or raw material or a warehouse of resources for us to use as we see fit. This is not what the Bible teaches!

It is important that we have a biblical view of the earth, especially in these days of growing concern about creation and the ecological crisis that threatens the handiwork of the Creator.

The Earth Is Good, Not Evil

Many of the psalms affirm this key teaching—the earth is good. "The earth is the LORD'S and everything in it, the world, and all who live in it" (Psalm 24:1). Genesis 1:1-13 and 1:31 give us the basic biblical teaching here. God pronounced the first light of creation "good" (Genesis 1:4). And having created the earth and the whole universe, "God saw all that he had made, and it was very good" (Genesis 1:31).

Because the earth is good, it is proper and even spiritual to love the earth. God loves the earth! It is an expression of his goodness. We should love all that God has made and rejoice in it. This is what the psalmist David does over and over again in the book of Psalms.

But here we face a problem. Are "the earth" and "the world" the same thing? Doesn't the Bible tell us, "Do not love the world or anything in the world" (1 John 2:15)? Yes, it does. And yet it also says, "God so loved the world" (John 3:16). So we have a little explaining to do.

This seeming contradiction goes away if we remember two points.

1. The Bible never forbids our love of the earth. When it says not to love the world, it doesn't mean the creation, nature— what God has made. There is nothing wrong with loving the earth. There's nothing wrong, in fact, with loving all the beautiful things that are part of earthly existence, including gardens, art, music, or even good, wholesome entertainment. This is why the apostle Paul says, "Whatever is true, whatever is noble, whatever is right, whatever is pure, whatever is lovely,

whatever is admirable—if anything is excellent or praisewor-
thy—think about such things" (Philippians 4:8).

It is all right to love the earth, to enjoy it, as long as we first
of all, deeply and continually, love God with all our heart and
mind and soul and strength, and our neighbor as ourselves.

2. The Bible says we should not love the sinful world system—that is, the corrupted set of values that have become
dominant in the world, and the twisted, tainted things that have
come from these wrong values. We should not love the sinfulness of the world. Yet we should love the world as God does.

In the New Testament, the word for "world" is usually the
Greek word *cosmos*, which, of course, is the source of our
English word *cosmos*. It can have several different meanings.
In the Bible, when the word *cosmos* refers to the world God has
made, including all its peoples, the world is the proper object of
our love. But when it refers to the corruption that is in the world
because of sin, then in this sense we should *not* love the world.

But we need to be clear that the world, as the physical
creation, is not evil. It is God's good work, the result of his
wonderful creative genius. In this sense, we can and should love
the world. We should cherish the earth.

This leads, however, to our second truth, which will help us
determine to what extent this planet is our home: the earth is
diseased and disordered because of sin.

The Earth Is Diseased and Disordered because of Sin

Romans 8 puts this graphically. It says that the whole creation
has been "subjected to frustration," that it is in "bondage to
decay." In fact, all of creation *groans* "as in the pains of childbirth"!

Can you picture that? The earth groans in its bondage, like a
pregnant woman groaning to deliver her baby—an image of
pain. And yet this image also contains hints of hope.

The point is, the earth is not in its normal state. It is not as
God created it. It suffers the effects of sin—not its own sin, of

course, because the earth cannot sin—but the effects of human sin.

How did this happen? We don't know for sure. There is a mystery here. In some way, the Fall of Adam and Eve disordered the whole creation. There are many hints of this in Genesis. The picture of the environment in the first few chapters of Genesis is much different from what we see following the Fall and the Flood. The dialogue of science and Scripture may someday help us to understand this better. But clearly after the judgments of Genesis 3 and 6, we see increasing disorder, shortened life spans, and a partially ruined, yet still beautiful earth. We see a created order "in bondage to decay."

The point is, human sin spoils the earth. It makes it suffer. In the biblical picture, men and women sin not only against God but also against one another and against the earth.

The Old Testament speaks about this in several different ways. Repeatedly God warns that if his people are unfaithful to his covenant, the land will suffer. Note, for example, the warnings in Leviticus 26 of what will happen to the land, the environment, if the people ignore God's gracious jubilee provisions. The Bible pictures a profound spiritual-physical-moral-ecological interrelationship throughout the created order. This is pictured perhaps most graphically in Hosea 4:1-3:

Hear the word of the LORD, you Israelites,
    because the LORD has a charge to bring
    against you who live in the land:
There is no faithfulness, no love,
    no acknowledgment of God in the land.
There is only cursing, lying and murder,
    stealing and adultery;
    they break all bounds,
    and bloodshed follows bloodshed.
Because of this the land mourns,
    and all who live in it waste away;
the beasts of the field and the birds of the air
and the fish of the sea are dying.

One would think the writer was living in the late twentieth century!

The biblical picture (as several scholars have shown in recent decades) is not only the story of God and his people. It is the story of God, the people, and *the land*. As you read the Bible, notice all the references to "land," and you begin to get a sense of this. And remember that in Scripture, in most cases "land" and "earth" are translations of the same original word. (In the New Testament, the Greek word *gé* is the root of our words *geology* and *geography*.)

Thus the Bible shows us that mistreating the earth is one of the clearest evidences of human sinfulness. We continue to sin against the earth—God's creation!—when we pollute the earth, waste the earth's resources, or fail to practice good stewardship of the land entrusted to our care.

Recently I heard a vivid example of this. A friend of mine, Ezekiel, grew up in a small village in Zimbabwe. As a child he enjoyed the clear stream, the hills and trees, the birds and animals. As an adult, he moved away and for political reasons was unable to return to his hometown for many years. When he did finally return, he was shocked and saddened. The stream was polluted, some of the wildlife had disappeared, and the people were impoverished. What had happened? The government had introduced new farming techniques that depended on fertilizer. At first, crop yields increased. But then an economic depression hit. People couldn't afford to buy the fertilizer. Land that had been overfarmed eroded, and yields dropped. The life of the whole village and much of the surrounding countryside was in shambles, decay. Instead of working harmoniously *with* creation, the new techniques ruined it.

As this example shows, the current crisis in creation is political, as well as personal and social. If we believe we should support policies that are *pro-life*, we certainly should also support policies that are *pro-earth*. We need a pro-life ethic that respects the life of the earth, as well as human life—and this for two reasons: first, because God made and loves the earth;

second, because *all our life and health*, physically speaking, depends on the health of the earth.

When I look at the earth, I see both beauty and sadness. As God's handiwork, it is truly beautiful, wonderful. But because it is subject to decay and destruction on account of our sins, it is in bondage. And that is the sadness that marks our earth. It is a sadness that should capture the attention of all God's people, even as we long to see the liberation of the earth that Romans 8 talks about.

This, then, is the second key thing we should remember—the earth is diseased and disordered because of sin.

The Earth Is Our Responsibility as God's Stewards

The Bible teaches a third key lesson about the earth. The earth is not just God's responsibility; it is *ours also*. God has placed us on the earth to take care of it.

This is clear from Genesis 1 and 2. Man and woman, together, are to care for the earth God has made. This is the first great commandment of stewardship that God gave to us, and it has never been revoked. Sin did not cancel this commandment. Rather, because of sin, this type of stewardship is needed all the more. Humankind has massively failed to fulfill its stewardship of the earth. We have done to the earth what we have done to each other: exploited, harmed, oppressed, raped, and ravaged. This is a matter of disobedience to Almighty God. The proper response begins with humble confession and is followed by repentance, which leads to more fruitful discipleship.

Stewardship means taking proper care of something, having been entrusted with this responsibility by someone in authority. This is a basic biblical theme. In the Bible, we see that stewardship is not just about time and money. In fact, there are two great areas of stewardship, according to the Bible: (1) the stewardship of creation, of all the world God has made and given us, and (2) the stewardship of God's grace. First Peter 4:10 tells us that we should be "good stewards of the many-colored grace of God" (a literal translation). Here is our great, fundamental stewardship: properly using and caring for the material world, and being faithful, responsible channels of God's grace to us in Jesus Christ.

As Christians, we often are lopsided here. We may fail to show as much concern for the earth as God does. Yet this is a fundamental part of our stewardship.

How shall we fulfill our stewardship of the earth? This concern has local, regional, national, and global dimensions. The science of ecology reminds us that all these dimensions are interrelated. So it becomes a part of our task as Christian congregations to ask what Christian faithfulness means in all these areas. Congregations, or small groups within congregations, can begin by taking inventory of the ways our lives already do touch all these dimensions, and of what faithful stewardship would mean in each one. We need to ask ourselves, What would God have us do to care for creation in a way that would glorify him?

Remember, our question here is stewardship of the earth. I'm not talking here just about the land, the soil. I'm talking about the *whole* earth, the whole planet—in fact, the whole created order. How we treat the planet is of concern to God. It is part of our stewardship, part of what it means to be disciples of the Lord Jesus Christ.

Our actions in this area can be real, genuine ministry. A biologist friend of mine teaches at a Christian college in the Midwest. He was given responsibility for a piece of woodland some miles from the college campus. Over the years he has been working to practice good stewardship principles when managing this piece of God's creation, while also using it as a learning center. Biblically speaking, this is a vital form of Christian ministry! He is working to show what reconciliation through Christ means for the created order. This woodland is a small demonstration plot of the kingdom of God, a small sign of the "reconciliation of all things" that God is bringing.

This is not just a Christian concern, however. God gives *all* human beings, not just Christians, stewardship responsibilities for the whole earth. This responsibility comes from the beginning of creation (Genesis 1:28). This is one reason why Christians should gladly cooperate with non-Christians, secularists, or people of other faiths when it comes to caring for the earth. We need not shy away from this vital cooperation. Whether they recognize it or not, non-Christians who care for creation are, at least in this area, doing the work of God.

The third great truth, then, is that we all must be responsible stewards of the earth.

The Earth Will Be Judged and Restored

Here is the fourth and final truth: The earth will be judged and restored. The finale of the story of our earthly home is in God's hands.

Notice the promise of Romans 8:21: "The creation itself will be liberated from its bondage to decay and brought into the glorious freedom of the children of God." An amazing promise! Just as we will be saved, *so also* the earth is to be saved—that is, "liberated from its bondage to decay." Just as we will be saved from all the effects of sin so also the whole creation will be saved from the effects of sin. Actually, this makes a lot of sense. How could our God be almighty and leave any traces of sin in our universe? If he called it all "good" at the beginning of time, then wouldn't he want to redeem it at the end of time? What a cause for wonder, meditation, and praise to God!

In the Bible, we see two recurring themes with relation to earth's destiny. One is judgment. The other is restoration. These are not contradictory because both center in the work of Jesus Christ. They're part of the same story. Jesus is both the Judge and the Liberator or Savior. We know this, of course, with regard to our own sin. But the same thing is true with regard to the whole creation.

The New Testament teaches us that the "model" of what God is doing in the created order, as in our own lives, is the resurrection of Jesus Christ. What God has done in Jesus he is doing in us and in the whole created order. He is judging and he is restoring, so that even "the creation itself" will come to enjoy "the glorious freedom of the children of God"!

As Christians, we confess our faith in the resurrection of the body, not just the survival of the soul. We believe that Jesus rose again physically and materially, not just spiritually or figuratively. Jesus' resurrected body was renewed and glorious, but it was the same body. And we know the same thing will happen to all who have become "new creatures" through Jesus Christ.

The amazing thing here is what it says about material existence—things like hands and blood, cells and molecules, rocks and quarks and protons. Somehow these too will be "resurrected," it seems—but each according to its kind, as Paul suggests in 1 Corinthians 15:35-44. Perhaps we can speak of the "death" and "resurrection" of the whole cosmos! But as with human beings, so with the cosmos: the death is not a destruction. Rather, it leads to a resurrection. Surely, this too makes a lot of sense. Could Almighty God ever be defeated by death? His power is displayed in creation; will it not also be displayed when he restores his glorious handiwork?

Two centuries ago in England, John Wesley had a profound sense of this. One of his favorite phrases was the "restitution of all things," a phrase found in the King James Version of Acts 3:21. In that passage the apostle Peter tells us, under the inspiration of the Holy Spirit, that the time is coming when God will "restore everything, as he promised long ago through his holy prophets." And so Wesley wrote:

> While "the whole creation groans together" (whether men attend or not), their groans are not dispersed in idle air, but enter into the ears of him that made them. While his creatures "travail together in pain," he knows all their pain, and is bringing them nearer and nearer to the birth which shall be accomplished in its season. He sees "the earnest expectation" wherewith the whole animated creation "waits for" that final "manifestation of the sons of God": in which "they themselves also shall

be delivered" (not by annihilation: annihilation is not deliverance) "from the" present "bondage of corruption, into" a measure of "the glorious liberty of the children of God."

Referring then to Revelation 21, Wesley notes in his sermon "The General Deliverance" that the promise of the destruction of death, evil, and pain is not restricted to humankind. Rather, we may expect that "the whole brute creation will then undoubtedly be restored, not only to the vigor, strength, and swiftness which they had at their creation, but to a far higher degree of each than they ever enjoyed." Then will be fulfilled the great promise of Isaiah 11:6-9.

Romans says the creation was "subjected to frustration, in hope that it will be liberated from its bondage to decay." *In hope!* There is hope for the earth.

As Christians, then, we can and should have hope for the earth, as well as our hope of heaven.

Whenever we plant a seed, whenever we see a fallen bird, whenever we gaze at a mountain, whenever we see a polluted river, *we hope* for the liberation of the whole creation, the great promise of which Romans 8 speaks.

The book of Revelation presents a wonderful picture of this liberation—judgment, but also liberation. Revelation 11:18 says, "The time has come for judging the dead, and for rewarding your servants the prophets and your saints and those who reverence your name, both small and great—and for destroying those who destroy the earth." Yet it also speaks of a new heaven and a new earth. The picture of the last chapters of Revelation is really a picture of God's creation, liberated and restored.

Is this heaven or earth in Revelation? The point is, it seems to be both! It is the joining of heaven and earth. Read Revelation 21 and 22, where the heavenly Jerusalem descends to earth. This is all part of the new creation that we await and for which we eagerly hope. The earth will be judged and restored as part of God's great plan of salvation.

Conclusion

"The earth is the Lord's, and the fullness thereof; the world, and they that dwell therein" (Psalm 24:1 KJV).

This is the deepest reason why we should care for the earth. Nothing in the New Testament suggests that the biblical concern for creation was canceled by the coming of Christ. Quite the opposite. In the risen Jesus Christ, we see the first fruits of a renewed creation, the promise of creation restored. So we must seek God's help to be faithful earth keepers today.

This is God's world. It is also our world, but only in the sense that we are stewards of and enjoy the good creation of God. We do not own the earth. How often do we claim that everything we have belongs to God? Surely, it should not be too difficult for us to acknowledge that the earth is not for our private ownership. There really is no such thing as "private property" in the biblical world-view because God is the owner of everything.

So we see, then, these four great truths in the Bible concerning our earthly home:

1. The earth is good, not bad.
2. The earth is diseased and disordered because of sin.
3. The earth is our responsibility as God's stewards.
4. The earth will be judged and restored.

How should this make a difference in the way we, as Christians, live?

1. We may enjoy God's good creation and praise God for it.
2. We may live before the world as good stewards of the earth. Christians should be at the forefront of modeling good stewardship principles, including care of creation. Minimally, this certainly includes recycling, healthy eating, and supporting sound environmental policies in government and business.
3. We may honor and support those Christians whom God calls to a ministry to the earth.
4. We can teach and model earth stewardship to our children.
5. We can continue to study Scripture to learn what it says about the earth. For too long, many vital texts have been over-

looked by the church. We can correct this blind spot by searching out God's vision for the earth.

> The creation waits in eager expectation for the sons of God to be revealed. For the creation was subjected to frustration, not by its own choice, but by the will of the one who subjected it, in hope that the creation itself will be liberated from its bondage to decay and brought into the glorious freedom of the children of God.
> —Romans 8:19-21

Praise the Lord!

Part Two

Isn't Our Primary Calling to Fulfill the Great Commission?

I have a Christian friend who is committed to earth keeping because he believes it is a central part of Christian discipleship. He also does not shy away from rubbing shoulders with secular environmentalists.

One day, Allan attended an environmental conference where each person was given two to three minutes to share about his or her work. Eventually, boredom and restlessness took over the meeting. Monotony grabbed center stage. The group's facilitator shifted anxiously in her chair.

When Allan took his turn to speak, he began with the honest claim—"I am involved in the environment because I am a Christian and this is a significant part of my faith." Monotony and boredom abdicated, and a stunned silence took charge. The facilitator whispered to Allan, "Forget about the two-minute time limit; take all the time you need!"

It may be that Allan broke the boredom by being a novelty, but I am convinced that our secular world is dying—literally and figuratively—to see Christians take a relevant stand on an issue that much of the church has scorned. Perhaps this is why some environmentalists drift toward New Age and Native American religions. If the church has no answers, then why not look somewhere else?

The sermons in Part Two show us how evangelism and

creation care are connected. They also remind us how desperately our world wants to hear about the Creator God and his Son, Jesus Christ.

A Bridge over Troubled Waters. Kevin Graham Ford believes that an entire generation is waiting for the church to take a relevant stand on environmental issues. He knows that this savvy generation will not participate in a Christianity that has few answers to the environmental challenges facing us. This sermon challenges us to model a vibrant Christianity to members of Generation X, so that they will be attracted to this faith. Ford speaks with authority, for Generation X is his own.

A Second Touch. What about missions? The missionary movement has been one of the hallmarks of biblical Christianity. Are creation care and Christian mission compatible? Stan L. LeQuire's answer serves as an appeal to all Christians who would be faithful to the privilege of being Christ's witnesses.

The Works of the Lord. John Stott's commitment to the proclamation of the gospel is widely respected. If anyone can explain the connection between mission and earth keeping, it is Stott. In this deeply biblical sermon, he affirms that authentic church ministry must include creation care as surely as it does worship and witness. In fact, Stott ably shows that creation and salvation *are* closely related, that Christian witness must consist of making known *all* the acts of God—both in creation and in redemption.

A Bridge over Troubled Waters

Kevin Graham Ford

For he has rescued us from the dominion of darkness and brought us into the kingdom of the Son he loves, in whom we have redemption, the forgiveness of sins. He is the image of the invisible God, the firstborn over all creation. For by him all things were created: things in heaven and on earth, visible and invisible, whether thrones or powers or rulers or authorities; all things were created by him and for him. He is before all things, and in him all things hold together. And he is the head of the body, the church; he is the beginning and the firstborn from among the dead, so that in everything he might have the supremacy. For God was pleased to have all his fullness dwell in him, and through him to reconcile to himself all things, whether things on earth or things in heaven, by making peace through his blood, shed on the cross.

—Colossians 1:13-20

Several different generations currently coexist in the United States. Each has its own attitudes toward the environment.Those of the GI generation, who came of age during the Second World War, are the movers and shakers. They are builders who learned how to survive in battle and in business. In Christian circles, they were the pioneers of the great parachurch movements, such as World Vision, Campus Crusade for Christ, and the Billy Graham Evangelistic Association. From a young person's perspective, it is the GI generation that has exploited the environment for the sake of "progress."

At the end of World War II, the United States experienced the greatest population growth in its history, the well-known baby boom. As baby boomers came of age in the sixties and seventies, they rocked the country with their music, their protests, their sexual revolution, and their idealism. Today, they are rocking the American church with "seeker-targeted" services, megachurches, and contemporary worship styles. When it comes to the environment, they seem to talk out of both sides of their mouths. On the one hand, they love a good fight, and so they protest "environmental exploitation." On the other hand, they appear narcissistic to the younger generation, and they seize every opportunity to make a buck at the expense of anyone or anything else.

In the early sixties, the boom became a bust, and the population growth of the forties and fifties was stunted. The resultant generation has been dubbed "baby busters" by some demographers. This is a generation that has grown up cleaning up the trash of the other generations. This is my generation. To generalize, we are angry and pessimistic. We distrust authority and programs. We blame the system—especially the government and the church—for our problems. When it comes to the environment, we blame the previous generations for the hole in the ozone layer and global warming. And we are concerned about the environmental problems that face us in the coming years. But we are not given to protest like our boomer predecessors. Rather, we prefer to take care of our own problems in our own way. Many people have written us off and have said that we will never amount to anything. They say we are incorrigible and unreachable. I beg to differ. My generation will emerge through the chaos and the rubble and bring about change. My generation can be reached. And one vehicle with which to reach us is a careful stewardship of creation. A bridge can be built to us by a vibrant and biblical care of creation. If we ever saw such an honest and dedicated effort to address the environmental crisis, we would stand up and take notice. But before we examine ways to reach my peers, we must first understand them.

Talking about My Generation

Baby busters. Generation X. Thirteenth Generation. Thirteeners. Slackers. Baby bummers. Most of us have heard at least one of these labels. But most of us who are members of this generation dislike all of them. If there is one common theme among my peers, it is this—*"Don't label me!"* However, in order for us to have any kind of meaningful dialogue, we need to use some kind of label. So, I will use several of these labels sparingly. Xers were born sometime from the early to mid sixties, through the late seventies and early eighties. The concept of "generation" is simply a shorthand sociological construct, so assigning precise dates is not very helpful. I am using this one lens to view a variety of macrocultural influences.

How do we see the world? This is a very important question because the answer to this question is also the answer to the question of how we perceive reality itself. Our world-view tends to be defined in negative, rather than positive, terms. The creeds of even Christian busters begin with "I do not believe . . . ," rather than "I believe. . . ." We are defined more by what we are not ("Don't label me!") than by what we are. Three underlying assumptions shape our worldview:

• *The world is not simple.* There is too much bureaucracy and not enough efficiency. We have grown up with too much red tape from an ineffective government.

• *The world is not user-friendly.* For us, there are few jobs waiting and little hope for advancement in those few jobs. We are left to our own resources to make it.

• *The world has no rules.* Many of us were brought up by parents who wanted to be our buddies rather than our parents. They imposed little structure and gave us few clear answers. So our world has no boundaries. As a result, some of us live apart from the traditions and rules of "the system."

These three underlying assumptions give rise to two recurring themes among Xers: *survival* and *risk.* We don't doubt that we will have food and shelter. But we do worry about surviving at the same standard of living with which we grew up. In fact, 78 percent of the baby busters I surveyed agreed with the statements, "The real world seems difficult. I am worried about finding a job, surviving economically, environmentally, or in other ways." As a result, we become risktakers. We are more willing to take risks than our elders were because we have less to lose and more to gain. This risk-taking attitude also impacts our recreation, our studies (the majority of Xers have cheated on exams), and our sexual encounters, despite the threat of AIDS. Why? Because there seems to be no tomorrow for us. Why not take a risk? Look at what kind of world we have been left with.

From 1973 to 1990, the real median income of families whose head of household is under the age of thirty dropped 16 percent, compared to a significant rise in the real median income of the rest of the population (source: U.S. Census Bureau). We are moving home to live with Mom and Dad because there are fewer good jobs available for us than there were for the baby boomers. Our generation has watched the national debt soar to four trillion dollars. The economic future is dim.

We have inherited a world that seems to be falling apart. We have seen leadership in every arena fail. We grew up with Watergate and the Iran Contra scandal. We grew up with Jim Bakker and Jimmy Swaggart. We grew up with junk bonds, Leona Helmsley, and Donald Trump. We grew up with the highest divorce rate in history. We were educational guinea pigs, thanks to the proponents of "open education." Is there any wonder that we Xers are cynical?

Last, but definitely not least, we've inherited an environment that has been exploited by the developed countries for the sake of convenience. The self-indulgence of the most recent generations has left us with a potentially dangerous environmental situation. The future of the environment seems bleak. Is it any wonder that we don't trust anyone else to clean up the environmental mess?

Why Ask Why?

What do Xers think about their world and their future? In fact, how do we think? More than anything else, the answer to this question is what separates us from previous generations. This also needs to be one of the primary considerations when presenting the gospel through a concern for the environment, as I'll explain later. We dress differently, act differently, and talk differently. But most of all, we think differently. My generation is the first postmodern generation. Without dwelling on the academic, allow me to give a brief description of postmodernism.

According to Stan Grenz (Carey Hall/Regent College), the modernist era was a combination of Enlightenment thinking and the Renaissance view of humans. Reason (eventually the scientific method) was the sole judge of reality. During the Enlightenment, the quest for reason dethroned the church from its seat of power to determine reality. In the Renaissance, the autonomous self replaced God as the center of existence. In short, the modernist era gave us reason "plus autonomy"—the "reasoning individual."

In postmodernism, however, both reason and autonomy have been under attack. From Einstein's theory of relativity in science to the deconstructionist notion that words have no inherent meaning in literature, postmodernism assumes that there is no rational, objective truth. As a result, "thirteeners" have been brought up with the notion that there is no truth. The church is wasting its time demonstrating the logical fallacies of relativism. Postmodern thinkers agree that there is no such thing as relative truth. They have abandoned the notion of truth altogether.

At the same time, a heightened emphasis on community has replaced the individual as the primary expression of what it means to be human. This has led thirteeners to believe that each community defines its own truth. What is true for *you* is not necessarily true for *me*. While this may seem like an impossible situation for Christians, postmodernism actually presents us with a golden opportunity! For centuries, we have battled science and modernism and lost many battles. Now, we are seeing that science cannot answer all the questions. The academic community is waking up to a reality that transcends reason. We are also seeing a trend toward community. Christians have always emphasized the absolute necessity of community. If handled properly, postmodernism prepares the way for biblical truth. If the church can respond properly, a great evangelistic opportunity can be claimed.

On the negative side, postmodernism has impacted the way we think about God. While 91 percent of us believe in God, 70 percent say there is no absolute truth. Xers view organized religion as a power play by the bunch of hypocrites leading the system. Due to cultural conditioning, Xers are less averse to terms such as "follower of Christ" and "Christian" than they are to terms such as "born again" and "evangelical," which carry negative connotations. The bottom line for busters is that we want to see a faith lived out with authenticity and integrity. Don't give us too much theology or theory. And you had better live what you preach. We want to see that Christ makes a difference in people's lives, in our society, and in the environment.

Bridge between Two Cultures

Many people decry the problems of this new generation—the violence, the laziness, the music, and the disrespect for truth and tradition. Whatever happened to the notion of "true truth"? How can we ever reach a generation that is so mystical? One answer is to look back to the New Testament and find the parallels between that culture and our own. Paul's letter to the Colossians is a wonderful starting point for bridging this gap. Perhaps, if we listen to this passage, we can build a new bridge to Xers.

Colossae was not the center of the ancient world. In fact, it was a rather small and insignificant city in Phrygia. Xers probably would have migrated to Colossae and other cities like it, had Xers been around at the time. Xers don't like the mainstream. Alternative bands are springing up in small cities like

Austin, Texas, and Chapel Hill, North Carolina. Xers try to avoid New York and Los Angeles. They feel comfortable on the fringes of society.

Additionally, Colossae's religious flavor was similar to that of postmodern America. Several religions were synthesized to form a new mystical religion. Elements of Judaism were blended with other elements of Phrygian culture—possibly mystery cults or Hellenistic mysticism. Xers live in a world of cafeteria-style religion. "Pick your favorite elements of each and put them on your plate, and that will be your religion for today." The influence of postmodernism and the influx of Eastern religion have given Xers a religion that is more mystical—albeit a tangible, not ethereal mysticism—than the rational religion of the Reformers. Xers, indeed, would have thrived in Colossae.

More than cultural links, however, we can find a bridge to the soul of my generation by looking at the biblical principles Paul gives us in Colossians.

Twin Mandates

God's two greatest mandates to human beings were to be stewards of creation and to participate with him in his work of redemption. Throughout the Bible we see these two themes inextricably connected. We find a promise of redemption in the creation story when God promises to bring salvation through Eve's child (Genesis 3:15). In the Ten Commandments, we read two accounts of the reason for keeping the sabbath holy. In one account, Moses links it to creation (Exodus 20:8-11), and in another, he ties it to redemption (Deuteronomy 5:12-15). In the primary text for this sermon, they are again bound together. We read in Colossians 1:13-16:

> For he has rescued us from the dominion of darkness and brought us into the kingdom of the Son he loves, in whom we have redemption, the forgiveness of sins. He is the image of the invisible God, the firstborn over all creation. For by him all things were created: things in heaven and on earth, visible and invisible, whether

thrones or powers or rulers or authorities; all things were created by him and for him.

No matter how hard we try, we cannot separate God's work of creation and his work of redemption. Paul makes it perfectly clear that the Logos, Jesus as wisdom personified, is the force behind both redemption and creation. I'm amazed that Christians have missed this for so long. Our presentations of the gospel have not touched on creation. We have overspiritualized the gospel and removed it from its earthly context. But we now have an opportunity to bring these two great mandates back together. We can use environmental issues as a port of entry for presenting the gospel to Generation X, if we can ever get over our fears of being labeled "New Agers."

I went to seminary at Regent College in Vancouver—a Southern boy with no understanding of what it meant to care for creation. I didn't understand why people got mad at me when I purchased paper plates from the grocery store during my first week. After all, being single, it was so much easier to do the dishes that way! And what was the big deal with using polystyrene foam cups for my coffee during study break? What kind of seminary was this? Were they into New Age stuff or what? Well, before long, I became convinced that God had called us to be faithful stewards of creation.

Over Christmas break during my second year at Regent, I attended an evangelism class at a seminary in another part of the United States. I was absolutely shocked to see classmates drinking coffee from polystyrene foam cups—even when the seminary had purposely put out real mugs! When I confronted someone about this, the person's retort was, "You're not going to give me that New Age mumbo-jumbo, are you?"

During my first year on staff with InterVarsity, we decided to order pizza for all forty staff members during summer camp. I looked in the cabinet of the kitchen and found thirty plates. Some members of our team thought that just wouldn't suffice, so they set out to buy paper plates. When I suggested that we use the real plates, they wouldn't budge. Finally, I volunteered with one of our staff directors to wash the dishes so that we woulun ... to buy the paper plates. To this day, one of my closest friends on staff insists that I've been influenced by New Age thinking!

Our first step when sharing the gospel with Generation X is to overcome our own fears. To our shame, we've let the New Age movement lead the way in caring for God's creation. A distinctly Christian responsibility has been taken over by people with little understanding of the Creator God. In our quest for "truth," we have reacted to the New Agers by going in the opposite direction. We must understand that caring for creation and participating in redemption go hand in hand. They are inseparable. And until my peers sense that the church is honestly concerned about caring for creation, they won't set foot in the door.

Random Motion

Several years ago, the alternative band R.E.M. put out a song called "It's the End of the World As We Know It." This statement is far more true than R.E.M. ever intended. Xers feel that previous generations have ruined our world —economically, politically, morally, and environmentally. Postmodernity has ended the supreme reign of reason in our world, as well. Modernists thought that we could explain everything about nature through reason. But quantum physics and the indeterminacy principle have opened the door for things that cannot be explained by reason. Physicists aren't sure what actually holds the world together anymore, leaving a vacuum waiting to be filled.

For some environmentalists, James Lovelock's Gaia hypothesis became a new gospel. Extrapolations from his theory have led some to believe that the earth, including every inhabitant and even the atmosphere, is a single, self-sufficient, and living being. This hypothesis has crept into the pop culture of Generation X, as my peers worship Mother Earth and claim that trees are theologically as important as humans. When Paul wrote to the Colossians, many of the Greek and Roman philosophers thought Zeus held the world together. Paul offered a corrective that was applicable then and still applies now—Christ "is before all things, and in him all things hold together" (Colossians 1:17).

Why have my peers not embraced Christianity? Many of my friends think environmental exploitation is a result of a Christian-based domination of creation. Lynn White, of course, is the most-quoted proponent of this view. Although White did not suggest renouncing Christianity, his attack on Christianity has led many others to reject Christian ideals. This rejection has opened the door to New Age philosophies and pantheism. When I began researching my book, *Jesus for a New Generation,* I discovered that my Xer peers had some unique definitions of spirituality. "Spirituality is climbing a mountain." "Spirituality is riding the crest of a wave." "For me, spirituality is going for a run late at night and feeling the cool breeze blow across my body." Xers, unlike boomers, are wary of mystical spirituality. But New Age philosophies have simply adapted to their surroundings. Xer spirituality has to be something that they can experience. Crystals and meditation don't cut it for them. At the same time, they can't believe in a God who would encourage humans to destroy the rain forests in Brazil or to rip a hole in the ozone layer for the sake of convenient transportation.

So, as Christians, we have a tremendous opportunity and responsibility. We must bring a proper theological perspective to the environment. We must instruct our brothers and sisters to be stewards of creation. At the same time, we must be willing to go to our nonbelieving friends with the truth. What holds the world together? How do we explain our complex universe?

Colossians 1:17-20 says:

> He is before all things, and in him all things hold together. And he is the head of the body, the church; he is the beginning and the firstborn from among the dead, so that in everything he might have the supremacy. For God was pleased to have all his fullness dwell in him, and through him to reconcile to himself all things, whether things on earth or things in heaven, by making peace through his blood, shed on the cross.

Jesus is the answer to the questions of postmodernity, just as he was the answer to the questions of modernity. In *him*, all things hold together. In *him*, our lives make sense. The world is reconciled in him, and we are reconciled to God through his blood.

The second step when presenting the gospel to Generation X is to use creation to point to a creator—the Creator. The world is visible to us. It is not *reasonable* to have a creation without a Creator, just as it is unreasonable to have a watch without a watchmaker. In postmodern apologetic, however, we can no longer persuade people through *reason* alone. We must be comfortable with the notion that some things are *beyond reason*. This, too, points to God. He is the mystery who holds the world together.

For most Xers, however, Christians have lost their voice. As Christians, we represent a system that has exploited the environment, kept women oppressed, and manipulated the poor. We must start over. We must each do our own part to fulfill the twin mandates of redemption and creation.

How do we win the right to be heard? One person at a time. Generation X is not interested in grand strategies or programs. Its members are less likely to give money to Greenpeace than they are to clean up the river down the street. They probably will not boycott the logging industry in the Pacific Northwest, but they are willing to help clean up a natural habitat.

It starts with Christians leading the way by recycling their waste. It means that we stop using polystyrene foam cups at our fellowship hours at church. We cannot buy the new convenient, disposable communion supplies that were advertised at the latest Christian Booksellers Association convention in Denver. My research indicates that Generation Xers in youth groups across the country are actually more interested in service projects than in ski trips! That means that we can have a day to clean up a portion of our nation's freeways. Our campus ministries can do the most effective evangelism not by approaching people with surveys in the cafeterias but by sponsoring "Earth Days" on campus and by building relationships with non-Christians in environmental clubs. By doing that, we will rub shoulders with our nonbelieving friends. We can work hand in hand with people of different religious beliefs. And they will see that Christians are leading the way to care for creation. And maybe, just maybe, they will see that our faith makes a difference.

My generation blames the environmental malaise on the system—not just on Christians. They are tired of being burned by the system and left to clean up someone else's mess. They are tired of bureaucracy. They are weary of empty and broken promises. Caring for creation is a God-given responsibility. At the same time, it is a wonderful opportunity to present the gospel in a relevant and practical way to my generation. But it will happen only through the hard work and discipline of millions of individual Christians. It cannot happen through lobbyists or political platforms. We just don't trust the system. Bob Pierce, the founder of World Vision and a member of the GI generation, had the right idea. "How do we change the world?" he asked. "One person at a time."

A Second Touch

Stan L. LeQuire

They came to Bethsaida, and some people brought a
blind man and begged Jesus to touch him. He took the
blind man by the hand and led him outside the village.
When he had spit on the man's eyes and put his hands
on him, Jesus asked, "Do you see anything?"

He looked up and said, "I see people; they look like
trees walking around."

Once more Jesus put his hands on the man's eyes.
Then his eyes were opened, his sight was restored, and
he saw everything clearly.

—Mark 8:22-25

Perhaps my most embarrassing moment as a human being
happened in the state of Maine, where I pastored a small Baptist
church. On two separate occasions, during biannual business
meetings, I found myself exceedingly bored. In both of these
instances, I absent-mindedly got my fingers stuck in the Communion cup racks that are found on the backs of the pews in
Baptist churches. My situation was most embarrassing during
those times when the congregation was called upon to stand to
sing a hymn. I would have to stand and sing like the Hunchback
of Notre Dame, since one hand was stuck in the cup rack. It was
most frightening, as well, because at night New Englanders turn
the heat off in their churches!

Today, however, my assigned topic is missions. Therefore, it
would be more appropriate to tell you the story of my second
most embarrassing moment, which happened on the mission
field. This happened at a church picnic in the nation of Côte

d'Ivoire, the Ivory Coast. If you have ever served overseas, you know what a challenge it can be to minister in a language that is not your own. I was obliged to use French in Côte d'Ivoire and was holding my own, but every now and then I would have to ask someone to repeat what he or she had said. At times, I would have to admit that I had no clue what someone was asking.

During this church picnic, Maurice came up to me and asked me a question in impeccable French. I was tired of saying, "I'm sorry, could you run that by me again." So, I decided that I would give Maurice an answer in spite of my ignorance.

"Yes," I replied.

Maurice was mortified. He asked, "Really?!"

Having gotten myself into a predicament, I decided to continue on to preserve my integrity. So, for the second time, I answered, "Yes!"

Again, Maurice: *"Really?!"*

"Yes!" I said. The tone in my voice expressed dismay that he wouldn't believe me.

Maurice could have been asking me anything at all: "Stan, do you like Lawrence Welk?"

"Yes!"

"Really?!"

"Stan, you bear a striking resemblance to PeeWee Herman. Is there any chance that you are related to him?"

"Yes!"

It is dumbfounding to imagine what he was asking me. And to this day, I have no idea what Maurice wanted.

I blew it.

It occurs to me that as we read Mark 8:22-25, some people might think Jesus "blew it." He touches a blind man with his own saliva. The blind man can then see, but Jesus must touch him a second time, as if some mistake had been made. Did the formula not work? Did Jesus not have enough faith?

I assume that you believe, as I do, that Jesus does not make mistakes. And if that is the case, then the message of this text is that the second touch of Jesus was part of God's plan all along.

Sometimes God works in this way: change and healing are part of a process. There are certain steps in a progression. At times, a second touch is needed.

My proposal to you is that as we take the gospel to the ends of the earth, we need God to touch us one more time. We are accomplishing wonderful things in the name of Christ, but a second touch is vitally needed because we struggle with color blindness, tunnel vision, and weak depth perception.

Color Blindness

After the blind man saw for the first time, he responded, "I see people; they look like trees walking around" (v. 24). This is a miracle! If Mark had ended his story with verse 24, we could all rejoice with a heartfelt "Hallelujah!" This is an amazing healing, to go from blindness to being able to recognize the human form.

But Jesus Christ wanted more for this man. It wasn't enough for the blind man to begin seeing people as walking trees. Jesus wanted him to see with color, clarity, and vividness. Therefore, a second touch was needed.

I believe that this is a picture for us in the church. We see many things well. I would be amiss to be overly critical. However, I do not sense that we understand all that God has for us. The color and vividness of the Great Artist is not apparent to us because we are somewhat hindered by "color blindness."

Perhaps some of you here today are veterans of Sunday school, as am I. In Sunday school, children get to do all kinds of wonderful activities, such as gluing cotton balls on blue construction paper to make puffy clouds. Some teachers teach children how to put beans behind damp blotter paper in jars. The kids watch over time as the beans sprout from the water, which, over time, stagnates in the jars. For many, the highlight is a Sunday in the spring or summer when the children are sent home with a wilting pansy crammed into a tiny pot.

Then the Sunday school student grows into adulthood, and for some reason these wonderful activities are forgotten. We

don't see adult Sunday school students gluing clouds on construction paper or growing beans. I believe that there is a
message in this! Could we be saying to our church members that
creation is for little kids? Creation becomes a cute story that
loses its relevance for mature Christians.

We are excluding parts of the Word of God that are full of
color and vividness. Over and over in Scripture, the glories of
creation are described. For the most part, however, these teachings remain forgotten in Sunday school and in the pulpit.

In Nehemiah 9:5-6, we read how the Levites commanded the
Israelites to rise to their feet to praise God:

> Blessed be your glorious name, and may it be exalted
> above all blessing and praise. You alone are the LORD.
> You made the heavens, even the highest heavens, and
> all their starry host, the earth and all that is on it, the
> seas and all that is in them. You give life to everything,
> and the multitudes of heaven worship you.

I sense that we have forgotten such vivid worship, worship
as proclaimed to us throughout Scripture. We have relegated
the glories of creation to preschoolers. As Christian men and
women, we need to remind ourselves that our Scripture begins
with the creation story, and I believe that as we do this, we will
reap many benefits. Our worship services will be renewed. Our
commitment to take the gospel to all nations will be deepened
because we will have even more reasons to speak of the glories
of the Creator God and his Son, Jesus Christ. We will *want* the
world to know of a God as glorious, colorful, and majestic as
our Maker, who is described in Scripture.

And evangelistically, I sense that we can accomplish great
things if we rediscover a few things that we have forgotten about
the Creator God. I have always wondered why it is that so many
environmentalists are not Christians. Environmentalism and
Christianity just seem to me to be naturally connected. They are
both so immersed in God's beauty. Could it be that the church
has been speaking to these people in drab, black-and-white
images like the ones the blind man sees in Mark 8:24? Are we

providing the world with tired, worn-out images of what it means to follow Christ—images similar to the stark, bare figures of trees in winter? Environmentalists are thirsty for color and vividness. They are waiting to hear from us.

Tunnel Vision

Jesus asked the man in verse 23: "Do you see anything?" And the man did! Even with the first touch, this man was well on his way to a miraculous recovery of his sight. Nonetheless, a second touch was needed for that man. I believe that a second touch is needed for the contemporary church, as well. A second touch might correct our "tunnel vision."

Perhaps the blind man in our text had a case of tunnel vision. The text is not that specific, but it may have been that this man could only see a limited area of space directly in front of him. His vision did not have the breadth he needed. He could make out the shapes of a few men like trees walking in front of him, but could he see the throngs of people gathered around to witness the acts of this young rabbi? The blind man could see a few people, but could he see the Pharisees on the periphery, who were muttering and trying to figure out what to do with this Jesus?

So Jesus touched the man a second time, and he was completely healed. Would that he would touch his church a second time, so that we could more effectively accomplish the commission he gave us!

I am a photographer. One of my favorite lenses is the wide-angle lens. This lens allows me to extend the edges of my photograph, so I have more in the image. This makes sense economically and aesthetically.

The church of Jesus Christ could learn a lesson or two from the wide-angle lens. We need a broader vision within the church. We are called to take the gospel to all people, even to the poor.

You may think we are already doing this. I will not argue with our accomplishments. It is simply my thesis that the church needs to go one step further to recognize the connection between environmental degradation and those who are in need. Many people suffering around the world are suffering because of what is happening to our planet. I do not sense that mission agencies have made this connection. They may be helping these people, providing them with water filters or improved agricultural techniques. But they have not made the biblical connection between the stewardship of creation and the suffering of the human community.

Human beings are suffering in profound ways because of what is happening to the environment. Environmentalists decry the spoilage of their favorite recreational beach. This is a tragedy, but there are people who need a cup of fresh water to make it to the end of the day. They are not interested in water for recreational purposes but as a matter of life and death. Environmentalists speak of what may happen to the air fifty years from now—and that is certainly a cause for concern. However, there are poor people on our planet who need clean air to breathe in the here and now. They are not concerned about air for the *future*, so much as air in the *present*.

The Word of God says: "He who oppresses the poor shows contempt for their Maker, but whoever is kind to the needy honors God" (Proverbs 14:31). There is a creation connection here. Our Creator is saying, "Yes, I made the mountains and the rain forests, but I made these people, as well, and you dare not oppress them."

Many of us "Anglo" environmentalists become attracted to this issue because of our love for hiking or fishing. This is completely understandable. However, our God who has made those mountains and fishing lakes is also the maker of the multitudes who suffer because our planet is being degraded.

You may think that as a representative of the Evangelical Environmental Network, I want to turn you into "green Christians." Perhaps you think that I want to paint Christianity a bright new shade of green. No, my interests lie in other areas. I just wonder if the church is being as biblical as it claims. I sense that we need another touch from the Lord so that we can recover the sense of worship that we have lost. I want God to touch the

church again, so that we might have a better understanding of
what justice means, so that we will be better equipped to take
the gospel to the ends of the earth.

Depth Perception

Once more, Jesus touched the man's eyes. What else did the
blind man need? What was in that second touch? Maybe he was
blessed with a new sense of color. Maybe the second touch
corrected his tunnel vision. Maybe he had a problem with depth
perception. Could he judge distance? He saw men as trees
walking, but were they ten feet away? One hundred yards away?
It may be that Jesus cured the blind man of weak depth perception.

Would that Jesus would touch the church a second time!
Certainly, the church has accomplished amazing things. Satel-
lite hookups allow us to proclaim the gospel to millions at a time.
Nations that once received missionaries from the West are now
sending out their own missionaries.

Nonetheless, I wonder if the church understands the depths
of the gospel of Jesus Christ. For the most part, we do. However,
a few verses give me pause when I consider their implications.
I share these with you now, not as one with all the answers but
asking you to meditate on what they might mean.

One of these verses is John 3:16: "For God so loved the world
that he gave his one and only Son." The word *world* is translated
from the Greek *cosmos*, which means the entire created order.
For God so loved everything created, that he gave his Son, Jesus
Christ. Supremely, he loves men and women, but God also loves
all of creation. What does this mean for our commission to take
the gospel to the world?

Colossians 1 contains several verses that refer to the creation.
Verse 23 reads, "This is the gospel that you heard and that has
been proclaimed to every creature under heaven." I would not
propose that we design "Four Spiritual Laws for Lizards." I would
not advocate the creation of another evangelical mission agency,
such as "the Evangelical Mission to Mice and Moose." However,

we do need to take a fresh look at verses such as these.

What is the connection between the cross and creation? It is my sense that Jesus hung there on the cross calling you and me to faith in him. When we believe in his mighty, life-changing act, the very ends of the earth are touched, affected, even rattled, by the salvation of our souls. I wonder if we really understand all that is meant to happen when we believe. Could it be that our lack of clarity on this matter limits the success of our missionary efforts? If we really understood how life changing, world changing the gospel is, if we really believed that our God is powerful enough to redeem not just human souls but everything, then maybe we would commit ourselves more fully to the task of taking this dramatic message to the ends of the earth.

Romans 8 says, "The creation waits in eager expectation for the sons of God to be revealed. . . . The whole creation has been groaning as in the pains of childbirth right up to the present time" (vv. 19, 22). The entire creation is waiting for a second touch to come upon the sons and daughters of God. A second touch would perhaps cure them of their problems with weak depth perception. Then they could see just how deep the love of God goes. It is truly miraculous that God can save the likes of you and me. However, divine redemption goes even further—to the very ends of creation. There is more to the gospel than we imagine. It is more powerful than our usual experience would lead us to believe. If the gospel has such power, do we not have all the more reason to preach it to the very ends of the earth? To tell everyone who will listen?

I am a Trekkie. I enjoy *Deep Space Nine* and *Star Trek: Voyager*. Whenever I meet someone, we go through the obligatory small talk about who we are, what we do, and what our families are like. But if I discover that the person is also "into Trek," then that person becomes so much more real and alive to me. Here is a decent human being!

How much more real and alive our God would become to us if we could recapture a sense of our maker's glories in creation—if we could understand just how broad God's love is for those who suffer, and how deep the gospel is that reaches to the ends of creation! Isn't the Creator more wonderful than we could ever imagine? Isn't he all the more worthy of our efforts to go to the ends of the earth? I believe so. Would that God would give us a second touch, that we might be all the more faithful to the task! Amen!

[This sermon was preached on March 15, 1995, in a chapel service for the students of Wheaton College, Wheaton, Illinois.]

The Works of the Lord

John R. W. Stott

I would like to add my congratulations and thanksgivings on this occasion of A Rocha's tenth anniversary. We are united in thanking God for the bold and imaginative vision that he gave the founders of A Rocha, an agency of Christians in conservation. A Rocha is committed to a partnership of Christian responsibilities—evangelistic, on the one hand, and environmental, on the other. It may be called "earthbound" in the double sense that it cares for the earth, and it is also concerned that the good news of Jesus Christ is carried to the ends of the earth.

I invite you to reflect with me on a phrase that occurs about a hundred times in the Psalter. Although I understand that the Hebrew words are somewhat different, nevertheless the idea is repeated again and again in the expression "the works of the Lord," the mighty works of Yahweh. What is vital to notice, because it is often missed, is that sometimes "the works of the Lord" are his mighty works of *creation*, bringing the universe into being and sustaining it by his Word of power. But at other times, the works of Yahweh are his mighty works of *salvation*, rescuing his people, Israel, from their slavery in Egypt and establishing them in the Promised Land. Both these works, of creation and of salvation, are said to be works of Yahweh. Let me give you an example of each.

The first, the works of creation, are described in Psalm 104:24:

> How many are your works, O LORD!
> In wisdom you made them all;

the earth is full of your creatures.

We read about his works of salvation in Psalm 40:5:

Many, O LORD my God,
   are the wonders you have done. . . .
Were I to speak . . . of them,
   they would be too many to declare.

The context of Psalm 40:5 is that the psalmist is being rescued from the horrible pit of sin and guilt, and his feet are being established upon the rock.

Now with this double understanding of the works of Yahweh in our minds, I want to ask the question, What is our Christian responsibility in light of and in response to the works of the Lord?

The Subjects of Our Study

First, the works of the Lord are to be the subjects of our study. Listen to Psalm 111:2 (RSV), to which I will refer again later: "Great are the works of the LORD, *studied* (NIV says "pondered") by all who have pleasure in them." Or Psalm 77:12: "I will *meditate* on all your works and consider all your mighty deeds."

I think it was Sir Francis Bacon, the seventeenth-century essayist, who was the first to say that "God has, in fact, written two books, not just one. Of course, we all are familiar with the first book he wrote, namely Scripture. But he has written a second book called creation." That is to say, God has revealed himself both in the created order and in Christ and the biblical witness to Christ. To be sure, there are a number of important differences between the two books of God, between the *general revelation* of his glory in nature and the *special revelation* of his grace in Scripture. Yet both are divine revelation. Now here is the point: What God has revealed, we are to study, to explore, to ponder, to meditate on, to make our own, and to rejoice in. We should be fascinated by the self-revelation of God and want to study his mighty works.

The seventeenth-century astronomer, Johann Kepler, said that when he was studying the universe, he was "thinking God's thoughts after him." Those words are equally applicable to Bible readers. Bible study and nature study are *both* Christian obligations, a necessary response to God's double self-revelation in creation and in Christ. This brings me back to Psalm 111:2 (RSV): "Great are the works of the LORD, studied by all who have pleasure in them."

These words were inscribed in the middle of the last century over the entrance of the old Cavendish Laboratory on Free School Lane in Cambridge. They were inscribed in Latin, in the Vulgate version, but when translated they say, "The works of the Lord are great, pondered by all those who delight in them." It is widely believed that these words were inscribed over the entrance to the laboratory at the instigation of the great physicist James Clerk Maxwell, who became the first Cavendish Professor of Experimental Physics at the University of Cambridge in 1871, when he was only forty years old. It was Maxwell who ushered in the new era of post-Newtonian physics. He was a Christian man; he believed in God the Creator. When he was only twenty and still a student, he affirmed his confidence as a Scot and a Presbyterian "that man's chief end is to glorify God and to enjoy him forever."

Now, when the New Cavendish Laboratory came to be built in 1976, less than twenty years ago, just off Madingley Road in Cambridge, it was, I understand, Christian influence that persuaded the authorities to inscribe the same text over the front door, this time in Coverdale's English: "The works of the Lord are great, *sought out* by all those who have pleasure therein." I have been very interested to discover that the very same text from Psalm 111 was the motto adopted by Lord Rutherford, whose pioneer work in nuclear physics led to the first splitting of the atom in the 1930s. These were Christian men, godly scientists, who were anxious not only to recognize the works of the Lord but to *study* his revelation. Bible study and nature study are twin obligations.

The Subjects of Our Worship

Second, the works of the Lord should be the subject, though not the object, of our worship. We are to rejoice in the works of the Lord, just as, we are told, he rejoices in his *own* works (Psalm 104:31). And when we rejoice in the works of the Lord, our rejoicing quickly slides into praising him for them. For God's mighty works in creation and salvation are to be the main subjects of our worship. It is not, I believe, an accident that Psalm 103 and Psalm 104 stand side by side in the Psalter, for they are beautifully complementary. Both of them begin and end with an invitation to praise the Lord. Psalm 103 (NIV) begins: "Praise the LORD, O my soul," and it goes on:

> . . . all my inmost being, praise his holy name.
> Praise the LORD, O my soul,
> and forget not all his benefits.
> —vv. 1-2

What are these benefits? The Revised Standard Version says:

> . . . who forgives all your iniquity
> and heals all your diseases;
> who redeems your life from the Pit,
> who crowns you with steadfast love and mercy.
> —vv. 3-4

In other words, it is praise of God the Redeemer.

Psalm 104 begins with the same words: "Praise the LORD, O my soul." Again we hear the invitation to worship Yahweh. But why should we worship the Lord?

> O LORD my God, you are very great;
> you are clothed with splendor and majesty.
> He waters the mountains . . .
> the earth is satisfied by the fruit of his work . . .
> The trees of the LORD are well watered . . .
> There the birds make their nests;

the stork has its home in the pine trees.
                                    —vv. 1,13,16,17

Psalm 104 is perhaps the earliest essay in ecology in the
literature of the world. It depicts the animals in their living
environment. Psalm 103 is an invitation to praise God the
Redeemer; Psalm 104 is an invitation to praise God the
Creator. In each case, we praise God on account of his mighty
works.

Now this double worship of God—for his mighty works in
creation and salvation, for his glory revealed in creation and his
grace revealed in Scripture—is only a stammering anticipation
of the full-throated chorus of heaven, in which angels, animals,
and humans will join in unison and sing:

You are worthy, our Lord and God,
    to receive glory and honor and power,
for you created all things,
    and by your will they were created
    and have their being.
                                    —Revelation 4:11

And again,

Worthy is the Lamb, who was slain,
to receive power and wealth and wisdom and strength
and honor and glory and praise!
                                    —Revelation 5:12

Thus the worship of heaven also recognizes the double nature
of the works of the Lord, as Creator and Redeemer.

The Subject of Our Witness

Third, the works of the Lord are to be the subject of our
witness. Worship and witness belong together. We cannot possibly worship God—that is, acknowledge his infinite worth—
without longing to go out into the world to persuade other people
to come and worship him. Worship leads inevitably to witness,

but witness leads to worship, too. It is a continuous cycle of worship leading to witness leading to worship and so on. The two cannot be separated.

In both worship and witness, the works of the Lord are paramount. Of course, we are used to the idea that we are to bear witness to what God has done in Jesus Christ for the salvation of the world. But the Scripture says we are also to witness to the wonderful works of our Creator. Here are two examples. Psalm 105:1-2 says:

> Give thanks to the LORD, call on his name;
> make known among the nations what he has done.
> Sing to him, sing praise to him;
> tell of all his wonderful acts.

And we hear in Psalm 145:4: One generation will commend your works to another; they will tell of your mighty acts."

So God's mighty acts in creation and redemption are to be made known throughout the world. I hope, sisters and brothers, that we will not be afraid to bear witness to the Creator, as well as the Redeemer. Just as the apostle Paul did when confronted by the philosophers in Athens, we need to hold together in our evangelistic witness the creation and the cross—the God who made us, and the God who has redeemed us in Jesus Christ. If either is omitted, our gospel has become truncated.

And so, I wish to conclude by encouraging those who honor the Lord by studying and pondering his works. I am thankful for those Christians who lead us to a deeper worship of the Creator God and who make known his works to others throughout the world—all to the glory of the one true God, Creator and Redeemer, the Father, the Son, and the Holy Spirit.

[This sermon was delivered at the tenth anniversary celebration of the A Rocha Trust on September 25, 1993, at St. Paul's, Robert Adam Street, London, United Kingdom. The Trust operates a vibrant mission that combines ecological field studies with Christian mission. The main center is located in southwest Portugal, where a field study center and bird observatory provide vital conservation education, while the members give witness to their faith in Jesus Christ.]

Part Three

Aren't Pandas More Important than People?

Radical environmentalism has earned itself a bad name. Many people, both Christian and non-Christian, are disturbed by what seems to be the environmentalist penchant for putting pandas and polar bears before people. The public seems to understand innately that humans have a unique role in creation. Perhaps we know this because it has been written on our hearts from the beginning of time. Certainly Christians know this because it is in the written Word of God.

As Christians proclaim God's revelation to an unbelieving world, we must hold fast to the truth that the human creation is just a little lower than the angelic (Psalm 8:5). This may make some environmentalists uneasy, but our calling is to announce God's Word faithfully, not to push "politically correct" ideas. In the end, our commitment to God's revealed truth will bear fruit because exalting animals can only demean humans. As this happens, we will lose the rationale for doing what is a distinctly human task: stewarding creation because we bear the image of the Creator.

Furthermore, as radical environmentalists overemphasize the needs of animals, they deemphasize the needs of humans. Millions of humans can't meet even the basic needs for clean air and clean water. Meanwhile, environmentalists preach about the needs of whales and birds. These are very real and worthy causes, but aren't the issues of human health far more important?

Again, this is where a "biblical environmentalism" can make a decisive contribution. One of the clearest themes in Scripture is God's concern for humans, particularly those who are poor, without a voice, and without the basics for a decent life, which God surely desires for them.

These three sermons provide a clear exposition of the witness of Scripture about caring for human needs, many of which are directly related to the degradation of God's creation. These sermons will compel. Some of them will unsettle. But perhaps the church needs this challenge to recommit itself to the vital mission of caring for the poor, those who suffer while creation groans.

Love Thy Neighbor. Myron Augsburger explains the many ways a Christian can live with compassion in a hurting world. He concludes with an impassioned plea for the church to recover its identification with the risen Christ, so that it may boldly proclaim the cross of Christ and the love of God in every aspect of life and work.

The Whole Gospel and the Broken World. Sharon Gallagher provides us with a helpful overview of the many crises that rip the human race to pieces. She then lays out a convicting challenge for God's people to live bold, authentic Christian lives. If we do this, we will not detract from the gospel's power to bind up the broken pieces of our world.

The Faces of Creation. Bob Seiple relates moving stories of people who suffer in times of natural disaster. He reminds us that we are not talking about public policy and global issues so much as about people, individuals, and often children.

Love Thy Neighbor

Myron S. Augsburger

He will faithfully bring forth justice.
He will not grow faint or be crushed
until he has established justice on the earth.
—Isaiah 42:3-4 (NRSV)

The good news of the gospel needs to be heard, understood,
and accepted by humanity. As we move into the twenty-first
century, the old story of the gospel remains vibrant, fresh, and
new! Futurists studying trends over time affirm that humanity
has experienced more change since 1935 than in all of human
history up to that time. Much of this change is good, but much
is not good. Whether it is or not, we are involved in the change
and are responsible for our actions in this change. We are
responsible for how the change affects God's creation and God's
purpose for his creation.

The modern world is now recognized to be a global community, and our thinking must shift to face this new reality. The
population increase to six billion has implications for relationships between nations, food production and distribution, education, economics, and so forth. With the increase in population
has come increased urbanization, and the concentration of people in cities has created yet more problems: assuring adequate
supplies of clean water, managing sewage disposal, and so forth.
Another factor is that a high percentage of today's global population consists of young people who have radically different
values from their forebears. Half of Mexico City's population
of twenty-four million is under the age of fifteen; that's twelve
million people who need to be influenced with the gospel of

Christ. But one of the greatest problems in our society is inequity, the injustice of the gap between the "haves" and the "have-nots" in our society. For many, this gap is about the extent to which people share in the benefits of creation—land, clean air, fresh water, and the like. We must be concerned to protect creation for the benefit of the poor and the coming generations.

We are told in Scripture to pass on the heritage of faith to the succeeding generations. The jubilee principle calls us to care for the created world for the generations to come. What a challenge! How can we speak of love to others without sharing with them the good news of Christ in word and deed, in content and character, in stewardship and in preservation? How can we live as Christ's ambassadors in a rapidly changing world? We must begin to live just lives with our neighbors and with all of creation.

Justice *Respects* God's Image in Humans

The two greatest commands of Scripture are to love God and to love one's neighbor. To love one's neighbor as one's self is to seek the best for one's neighbor, and doing so in love means that we accept the cost of sharing fully with the neighbor. One unique evidence of our faith is that we live in hope, and when doing so, we try to live out the purpose of God for his creation "until he comes."

In the early 1950s, I was pastor of a church in Sarasota, Florida. As an outreach from our congregation, we began a work in a community, known as New Town, on the north edge of the city. We built a building, engaged people in the new venture, and soon had a small congregation of people, black and white, worshiping together. This was before the civil rights movement, and such a project was not popular. One Sunday evening one of our young men was helping an elderly black gentleman home from the church service when he was arrested by a policeman, called a "nigger lover," and put in prison. By the time his pastor arrived the next morning, the young man was already in khaki pants and ready for the chain gang! In both black and white, the image of God was being demeaned. Christians must oppose such assaults on God's human creation.

In a 1963 conference at Howard University in Washington, D.C., John Perkins, speaking about African Americans, said that we cannot give people dignity; we just need to recognize it!

Recognizing the image of God in all people, we are called by Scripture to treat everyone with equal dignity: men and women, people of every race, rich and poor, educated and illiterate alike. God treats people with respect, regardless of their standing, and he expects us to practice a similar justice with one another.

Since we are all alike in having been created in the image of God, it is our Christian responsibility to treat one another justly, that is, to seek fairness and equity for each person. Human rights are a Christian responsibility. We are called by God to seek public justice, to work toward a consensus that can enable cooperative action, to care for the creation as God's provision for all people. The time to act is now. Our continued silence could make matters worse. Dr. Martin Niemöller, writing of his experiences in the concentration camp under Hitler, convicts us with these words:

> In Germany they came first . . . for the Jews, and I didn't speak up because I wasn't a Jew. Then they came for the trade unionists, and I didn't speak up because I wasn't a trade unionist. Then they came for the Catholics, and I didn't speak up because I was a Protestant. Then they came for me, and by that time no one was left to speak up.

Justice *Reflects* God's Nature

The Old Testament has many references to God as a God of justice. We read, for example, "For the word of the LORD is right and true; he is faithful in all he does. The LORD loves righteousness and justice; the earth is full of his unfailing love" (Psalm 33:4-5).

Our God is just, and God's people must reflect that justice. Jesus gave justice a prominent place in fulfilling the expectations of God for his people. He corrected selfish thinking when

he told the religious leaders that, although they were very careful
to pay the tithe of even the smallest vegetables of the garden,
they failed to observe "the more important matters of the law—
justice, mercy and faithfulness" (Matthew 23:23). These, he
said, they "ought to have practiced, without neglecting the
former."

Put quite simply, justice is a compassionate approach toward
people who are hurting and toward a creation that has been
degraded. It is love in action. "The earth is full of his unfailing
love." Can we say that our actions retain the fullness of God's
love? Do our lifestyles drain the planet of God's pure justice?

Justice *Rejoices* in Freedom

Freedom is where love and power meet in justice and righteousness. Each of us has to steward our personal power. The
question is, How will we use our power of personal influence,
our power of education, our power of resources, our power of
place? It is love that prevents power from becoming tyranny.
Power is used justly when it releases the potential and enables
the freedom of others by respecting the intrinsic worth of every
person before God.

In the spring of 1981, I was invited to address the Oakbrook
Executives Club at the Oakbrook Sheraton in Illinois. Arriving
at the O'Hare terminal the evening before, I stepped out on the
sidewalk and looked for the limousine to the hotel. While I
waited, I overheard two men near me speaking about a meeting
at the Sheraton, so I suggested that we get a taxi and split the
fare three ways. We did so, and the two men continued their
conversation for a while. Then the one man turned to me and
said, "Are you here for this agricultural equipment convention
tomorrow?" I replied that I was to address the Oakbrook Executives Club. The man asked me what the club was. I told him what
I knew about it, and then he asked, "What is your topic?"

I replied, "Love, Power, and Freedom."

He immediately responded, "They don't fit!"

I smiled and said, "It depends on your definitions. If you have power and not love, there will be no freedom, for there will be tyranny. But if you have power and have love, there will be freedom, for you will not violate your neighbor."

The man was silent for a moment and then responded, "Young man, if you could get that message across, you could change the world." And that is what I'm out to do, by exercising Christ's teaching on love and justice.

In 1947, General Omar Bradley, in an Armistice Day address, said, "Our humanity is trapped by moral adolescents. We have too many men of science, too few men of God. The world has achieved brilliance without wisdom, and power without conscience." His words well express our need for people of justice and righteousness, people who will find in their vocations a better way to care for God's creation and thereby serve him. For too long, we have used our freedom as a license to destroy and demean. A godly justice will rejoice in a freedom that can be used to express unconditional love.

Justice *Restores* Community

As members of the body of Christ, we care for one another, we respect one another, and we secure the freedom and right of one another for self-fulfillment in and with the group. This is a way of life that we learn from the Master. And with the global population higher that it has never been in history, we face a new ecological concern: resources must be stewarded for the good of all, now and for future generations. How will we demonstrate this respect, and how will we reflect the nature of God in a world where creation is increasingly degraded and where creatures are demeaned on a large scale?

Scripture has so much to say about being a good neighbor. Many of the passages are well known. For example, "Do not plot harm against your neighbor, who lives trustfully near you" (Proverbs 3:29). We remember, too, the second greatest commandment, "Love your neighbor as yourself" (Matthew 22:39). In this day and age, we need to ask ourselves again if we are doing a very good job of loving our neighbor. Can we say that we love our neighbor when our extravagant lifestyles will guarantee the poverty of those whom Christ loves? Can we say that we love our neighbor when we belch polluted air into their backyards? When we dump our waste into a stream? "Good riddance!" "Out of sight; out of mind." But that waste will wind up in someone's water supply. Is this what the Bible calls living as a good neighbor?

Justice is a community concern. We seek together to secure justice for each individual. By doing so, we also secure justice for the whole. This is a major contribution the Christian community can make to the unbelieving world. While we are citizens with one another in society, we are first of all citizens of the kingdom of heaven! As such, we take action as we boldly pray, "Thy will be done on earth as it is in heaven."

Justice *Reveals* Compassion

A major problem in Western society is the extent to which our individualism has isolated us from one another. The average American finds it almost impossible to share intimately with another. Intimacy involves trust, familiarity, closeness, and understanding. Intimacy means involvement with another person, the willingness to be vulnerable, an interest in sharing pain and defeat, as well as successes. There is no full justice apart from a depth of compassion that brings to another a sense of self-worth. Justice enables others to find their greater fulfillment; it is uplifting. Our mutual support is not a handout as much as a "hand up."

It is not easy to look with understanding at our own culture, because we are so close that we can't see the woods for the trees. Only when we take a step back from the culture of which we are a part can we analyze it and interpret the implications of compassionate justice for our common life. Here are a few exercises that might help you take a step back from our culture and think about the way we live our lives:

• Imagine yourself in the space shuttle looking back on your neighborhood and your country. What do things look like from such a distance? What do you miss? What really counts in your daily life?

• Imagine yourself as a visitor or a refugee from a distant country. What do you observe about your new home and life-style in the West?

• Recall a time when your neighborhood was transformed by a winter blizzard or even a brief power outage. What were your feelings at the time? How did your neighbors relate to one another? (Many people experience others becoming very friendly and neighborly during such challenging times. Some people even regret life returning to "normal" because the difficulty has provided a reminder of a different, and perhaps more rewarding, way of life!)

Justice *Reaches Out* in Mission

The call to Christian mission must be heard as a call to a mission of justice as one expression of spiritual fellowship. God's salvation means restoration for the whole of life. For Christian missions to emphasize the importance of physical healing and to seek miracles for such, while not being equally concerned for social and emotional healing, is hardly consistent. For missions to "reach down" to the poor and to offer them a salvation that promises eternal life, but then to fail to share the eternal quality of life in God's will *now*, is not the full gospel. To go out in mission, and at the same time to fail to seek social justice for those among whom we minister, is to lack genuine compassion.

In the spirit of Christ, we are called to pursue justice for the oppressed, to seek freedom for those who are in bondage, and to announce the time of the Lord's favor, the jubilee of restoration! The kingdom of God is among us, for the King is with us. We are heralds of the new word of grace, of the new quality of life, of the new community of the Spirit. Now there is neither Greek nor Jew, for he is our peace; he has broken down the barrier and brought to birth a new humanity, so making peace (Ephesians 2:14-18). Of this Messiah the prophet Isaiah said,

"In faithfulness he will bring forth justice; he will not falter or be discouraged till he establishes justice on earth" (Isaiah 42:3-4).

As Jesus' disciples, his ministers of reconciliation, we are involved in a mission of justice to provide equal opportunity to all, opportunity to come into God's family. We should love our local and global neighborhood enough to promote the kingdom of God and its values worldwide! We do this through the many Christian disciples who carry this expression of love and justice outside the four walls of their churches, into the orders of the common life. George MacLeod expresses this most effectively:

> I simply argue that the cross be raised again at the center of the marketplace as well as on the steeple of the church. I am recovering the claim that Jesus was not crucified in a cathedral between two candles, but on a cross between two thieves; on the town garbage heap, at a crossroads so cosmopolitan that they had to write his name in Hebrew, and in Latin, and in Greek, at the kind of place where cynics talk smut and thieves curse, and soldiers gamble. Because that is where he died. And that is what he died about. And that is where churchmen should be and what churchmen should be about.[1]

Many evangelical Christians are very reluctant to accept the fact that poverty for the millions is directly linked to injustice, to power struggles that increase the gap between the haves and the have-nots. It is also difficult for us to understand that so much human suffering is directly related to our abuse of God's creation. We need to hear the Master say to us, "I was hungry and you gave me something to eat, I was thirsty and you gave me something to drink, . . . I needed clothes and you clothed me, I was sick and you looked after me. . . . Whatever you did for one of the least of these brothers of mine, you did for me" (Matthew 25:35-40). In this awareness, the Lausanne Covenant says: "All of us are shocked by the poverty of millions and disturbed by the injustices which cause it. Those of us who live in affluent circumstances accept our duty to develop a simple lifestyle in order to contribute more generously to both relief and evangelism."

When the Christian church recovers an identification with the risen Christ that results in newness of righteousness and justice in action, the church will be relevant in society. But unless we see salvation as a present relationship that changes things for us both inwardly and outwardly, we will fail to participate in the full meaning of redemption.

When John 3:16 boldly proclaims, "For God so loved the world," we are to understand that God's love extends to the world, the *cosmos* (in Greek—the entire created order). Jesus' death on the cross is testimony to God's power to save human souls and to undo the effects of sin, wherever they might be found: creation, communities, institutions, and the like. The hour has come for the church to dig a little deeper, to discover just how mighty our God is.

[1] George F. MacLeod, "Only One Way Left," from *The Way of the Cross & Resurrection*, John M. Prescher, ed. (Scottdale, Pa.: Herald Press, 1978), 72.

The Whole Gospel and the Broken World

Sharon Gallagher

Jane Smiley's award-winning novel, *A Thousand Acres,* tells
the story of a family falling apart in rural Iowa. A farmer who
has spent his life adding acre to acre, making his land profitable
with quantities of toxic pesticides, decides to give his farm to
his three daughters. His decision initiates an ugly cycle of greed
and hostility. As the tight web of family secrets slowly unravels,
we learn that this man has used and abused his daughters, as
well as his land—he feels they are all his property to use as he
wants. All the while, he is enjoying the respect of his neighbors—because he's prosperous. In the end, his legacy to his
daughters is infertility and cancer. The poisoned farm is bought
out by an agribusiness that presumably will further pollute the
ravaged land. There is a church in the nearby town, but it seems
peripheral and irrelevant, with little impact on the moral life of
this family. The church issues no call for repentance and so can
offer no hope for healing. The story ends in bitterness, recrimi-
nation, death, and the disintegration of community.

Despite its debt to *King Lear,* Smiley's book is a uniquely
American story of the nineties, a time when tales of abuse are
rampant, when former unmentionables are public and common-
place—and when, at the same time, the myth of America's rural
heartland is badly tarnished.

The theme of *A Thousand Acres,* the relationship between
domination of the earth and domination of women, is a recurring
one within feminism. A related theme lays blame for this abuse
of power on Christianity. Since Lynn White's famous 1967

essay, "The Historic Roots of Our Ecological Crisis," it has become common wisdom among the "politically correct" that Christianity is responsible for the degradation of the environment. Since the inception of the secular women's movement in the late sixties and early seventies, Christianity has also been seen as providing a cultural rationale for sexism.

By the late seventies, the American women's movement could no longer accurately be called secular, although a general hostility toward Christianity still prevailed. Many feminists who felt shut out from what they saw as male-dominated religions began turning to goddess or nature religions in response. In a 1979 anthology called *Womanspirit Rising,* Carol Christ articulated their feeling: "Goddess symbolism undergirds and legitimates the concerns of the women's movement, much as God symbolism in Christianity undergirded the interests of men in patriarchy."

The feminist rejection of Christianity is especially unfortunate because the message of biblical Christianity is *not* negative toward women or the earth (although certain strains in Christian *theology* can lead to the conclusion that it is).

The influence of Platonic and Neoplatonic thought on the writings of early church fathers has perverted much biblical teaching on women and the earth. The Platonists envisioned a hierarchy of life in which mind and spirit were placed over and against matter (the body, the earth). In this system, women were associated with the earth and were assigned low status. Men, associated with mind and spirit, were at the top of the hierarchy and were given the right to rule.

Regrettably, much evangelical Christian theology is still dominated by that kind of hierarchical thought—with its legacy of unbiblical dualisms: male/female, spirit/flesh, faith/works. Let's take a look at each of these.

Male and Female

Platonic presumptions about the nature of woman emerge fairly undisguised in the writings of some of the most influential of the church fathers. Augustine, for example, interpreted 1 Corinthians 11:3-12 to mean that a man is forbidden to cover his head because he is made in the image of God, while woman is not made in that image (at least not physically), although her mind can be redeemed. Centuries later, Aquinas wrote that females were conceived because of a "defect in the active force."

This pagan antifemale bias not only influenced theological commentary; it also crept into Scripture translations. Since it was presumed that women were naturally unfit to be leaders, New Testament references to women were slanted by translators to obscure the fact that they *had* been leaders. For example, the Greek word *diakonos*, translated "minister" when applied to men, was translated "servant" when applied to a woman (see Phoebe, in Romans 16:1-2).

Of course, in this hierarchical thinking, if the male alone carried the image of God, it was also presupposed that God was male. Unfortunately, we're not talking ancient history here. In a 1993 *Christianity Today* article arguing against inclusive language, Elizabeth Achtemeier stated, "The Bible's language for God is masculine, a unique revelation of God in the world."

That kind of thinking has driven many women away from the church to search for a spirituality that has a place for them; it is also clearly contrary to biblical teaching about God's nature. In Genesis 1, we read that God created humanity in his image: "male and female created he them" (v. 27). God cannot be defined in human categories; however, both male and female humans reflect something about who God is.

While the Greek Platonists developed a hierarchy (in ascending order) of animals, slaves, women, and men, Jewish males later developed their own way of defining "the other." Orthodox men uttered a daily prayer thanking God that they were not created "a heathen, a slave, or a woman." Paul's great statement of equality in Galatians 3:28—"There is neither Jew nor Greek, slave nor free, male nor female, for you are all one in Christ Jesus"—directly repudiates that prayer. Yet Christian friends have told me that Paul's statement was meant in a spiritual sense, that this verse was not intended to affect how women are treated on earth. Only in heaven, they say, are we equal.

Flesh and Spirit

This spiritualized interpretation of Galatians 3:28 is one example of the Hellenization of Christianity that cut Christianity off from its Jewish roots and withered its ethical implications. Another effect of this spiritualization was to create a flesh/spirit dichotomy.

It is true that Paul encouraged Christians to "walk not after the flesh, but after the Spirit" (Romans 8:4 KJV). But what Paul meant by *flesh* was not earthiness, not our incarnateness, but our sinful natures. By *flesh,* or sinfulness, Paul was referring to that part of our nature that is selfish, greedy, lustful—the qualities that have, in fact, led to domination of women and to ruination of the earth. He was not saying that our bodies are evil, nor was he saying that we could develop a "spiritual" nature that is not incarnated in our behavior.

Biblical writers often remind us of our earthiness, that we are dust. In Psalm 103:13-16, in language that is both reassuring and humbling, we are told:

As a father has compassion on his children,
    so the LORD has compassion on those who fear him;
for he knows how we are formed,
    he remembers that we are dust.
As for man, his days are like grass,
    he flourishes like a flower of the field;
the wind blows over it and it is gone.

These biblical references to our beginnings remind us of our kinship with the rest of the created order. Our bodies are mortal, but they are not bad. They are part of the created world that God declared good. If we are open to God's Spirit, they can be elevated to become temples, places of worship (1 Corinthians 6:19).

Faith and Works

A disembodied spirituality often results in talk of saving "souls," without regard for the physical needs of these souls. Some Christians even argue that focusing on physical needs or social issues is opposed to the real work of the gospel.

It is sad that much of American Christianity is divided over this issue. On the one hand, many Christians who are concerned about evangelism and personal morality live as if they had never read the countless biblical injunctions about justice and peace and the poor. On the other hand, many Christians who live lives dedicated to promoting justice and peace behave as if the Bible doesn't speak to personal morality, and they seem, frankly, embarrassed by evangelism. Christians like John and Vera Mae Perkins, who have lived their lives ministering to the physical and spiritual needs of people while maintaining biblical moral standards, are the real witnesses to the gospel in our culture.

In the gospels, Jesus stated that those who know him would be distinguished from those who don't by their actions: the cup of cold water given in his name, sharing food and clothing, visiting the sick and imprisoned. "Whatever you did for one of the least of these brothers of mine, you did for me" (Matthew 25:31-46). In his epistle, James wrote that faith without works is dead (James 2:17). We cannot claim to love God without practicing love toward our neighbors. Jesus also told stories to illustrate these vital teachings. Let's look at three of them.

The Bad Steward

The parable of the bad steward (Luke 12:45-48) tells the story of a man who, in the absence of his master, misused his fellow servants and his master's goods. The servant said "in his heart, My lord delayeth his coming." Then that servant began "to beat the menservants and maidens, and to eat and drink, and to be drunken" (v. 45 KJV). When his master returned, the steward was punished for abusing what had been placed under his temporary authority.

Today, looking at humanity's "stewardship" of the earth, we

see the bad stewards not only recklessly destroying what isn't theirs—the water, land, and air that the Master created—but doing so suicidally, undermining the very things upon which their life and health depend.

Because they were animists, many preindustrial people treated creation respectfully, including the trees they felled and the animals they killed. Believing that nature was inhabited by spirits, they prayed after the hunt to appease the spirits of dead prey. In the West, animism has been generally banished by Christianity. In its wake, secular science has moved in, regarding nature only as object—data to be used and managed like numbers on a page. For Christians, however, animistic respect for animal and plant spirits should not be replaced with carelessness or wanton destruction but with a healthy fear of God and a respect for what belongs to God.

The Mustard Seed and the Leaven

The "bad stewardship" of some Christians today comes, in part, from the idea that God's kingdom is only heavenly. Jesus certainly reigns with God in heaven, but he also came to earth to inaugurate his kingdom. Those who know him are to behave in the radically different ways that Jesus modeled when he was here on earth.

In Luke 13:18-21, Jesus answers the question,"What is the kingdom of God like?" "It is like a mustard seed, which a man took and planted in his garden. It grew, became a tree, and the birds of the air perched in its branches." And, "It is like yeast that a woman took and mixed into a large amount of flour until it worked all through the dough." Jesus used organic images of cooking and gardening, not celestial images.

George Tinker, a Native American Christian theologian, has said that American Indians have a better ecological theology than Europeans because of the way they view the kingdom of God. The question Christian Native Americans ask is, Where?— *Where* is the kingdom of God?—while Europeans ask, When?—*When* will the Lord return? Some Christians, in their eagerness to leave this world, have spent much misdirected energy on speculative date setting. This apocalyptic perspective can lead to the attitude expressed by former Secretary of the Interior James Watt: Since it's all going to burn anyway, why not destroy America's wilderness reserves? Using the language of military conquest, Watt described his job as "occupying the land until the Lord returns."

The American Indian question, Where is the kingdom of God?, is the right one—and it is easier to answer. "Where two or three are gathered in Christ's name" (Matthew 18:20), there the ethics of the kingdom are to be lived out.

The World Needs Wholistic Solutions

The world's resources are being depleted and poisoned at an alarming rate at the same time that the world's population is exploding—clearly a formula for disaster. As we survey ecological problems around the globe, we see that they are related to issues of justice and peace.

In a recent *Atlantic Monthly* article, "The Coming Anarchy," Robert D. Kaplan describes the social disintegration and violence in West Africa that have followed in the wake of environmental degradation. He finds that for many young boys roaming the streets with rifles, war is a step up in their existence, since they started with nothing. Kaplan argues that natural causes, as well as social causes, are responsible for social and political upheaval. He concludes, "It is time to understand the environment for what it is: the national security issue of the early twenty-first century."

Kaplan's article also describes the impact of religion in African society. In North Africa, where the majority of the people are monotheists, Islam holds society together with a strict moral code, so that even in poor neighborhoods some level of human dignity is maintained. West Africa has not fared so well. An African Christian minister comments sadly about the region, "Western religion is undermined by animist beliefs not suitable to a moral society, because they are based on irrational spirit power. Here spirits are used to wreak vengeance by one person against another or one group against another."

In the West, where animism has been replaced by positivism, science—cut off from any value questions—has introduced other problems. It was value-free Western science that led to the most lethal ecological threat, the atomic bomb. It also led to an attempt to turn economics into "pure" science, apart from any human considerations. (I have met even Christian economists who espouse this.) With profit as the only goal, with no thought for the welfare of their workers or the larger community, unprincipled corporations have polluted and destroyed their environments.

Yet some of the most severe ecological damage of recent history has been sustained in Eastern Europe and the former Soviet Union, in countries that denounced unbridled capitalism. Unfortunately, these societies did not renounce warmongering. They did not spend what was necessary to control pollution; the health of their people and their land was subservient to the arms race. In the United States, the military has also produced enormous amounts of toxic waste. But here, at least, the mitigating effect of participatory democracy—angry, voting citizens—has prevented the degree of ecological suffering sustained by former Soviet bloc countries.

Just as ecological devastation in West Africa has led to war and violence, militarism has led to ecological devastation. We saw this most clearly in the recent Gulf War.

The Biblical Call to Wholeness

In Scripture, the issues of peace and justice are inextricably bound together with the health of the people and the land. The institution of the weekly sabbath day, the sabbatical year, and the year of jubilee are calls for people, land, and animals to rest. This is not only practical and health promoting; it is also a concrete reminder that we do not "own" land, animals, or other people. They are God's; we are stewards for a season. We read in Leviticus, for example, "The land must not be sold permanently, because the land is mine and you are but aliens and my tenants" (Leviticus 25:23). The injunctions in Leviticus also carefully spell out that slaves and aliens in the land are to keep the sabbath. God has instituted the sabbath to protect all people, regardless of class or race.

In Psalm 72, in the description of the righteous king, we again see that themes of justice, health, and peace are interwoven:

He will judge your people in righteousness,
    your afflicted ones with justice.
The mountains will bring prosperity to the people,
    the hills the fruit of righteousness.
He will defend the afflicted among the people
    and save the children of the needy;
    he will crush the oppressor.
In his days the righteous will flourish;
    prosperity will abound till the moon is no more.
Let grain abound throughout the land;
    on the tops of the hills may it sway.
Let its fruit flourish like Lebanon;
    let it thrive like the grass of the field.
          —Psalm 72:2-4,7,16

Conclusion

While we long for the kind of earth described by the psalmist, the earth we live in is being ravaged and poisoned. The society we live in is in crisis. Torn apart by racism, sexism, and poverty, it needs to hear the whole biblical message and see that message lived out.

We are told that a little leaven can leaven the lump. Like it or not, we are part of the lump: we live in human bodies of flesh, we live on the earth, we live in society. Perhaps if enough Christians lived, worked, and voted in ways that sustain the earth, we could preserve what remains of the good things God created. All to his glory!

The Faces of Creation

Bob Seiple

Let me begin with a story. The names are fictional; the circumstances, all too real; the destructive loss of life, an increasing fact of life.

Schmata is a twenty-four-year-old Bengali woman. At one time she was married with two children—Sharish, four years old, and Emil, two years old. Today she is a widow and, with a grief that most of us will never have to understand, childless.

It was the flood, normally not a big deal. Bangladesh always has floods. They are inevitable, most often predictable, and if someone really wanted to do something about them, probably fixable. But this one was different. The international press was already calling it the "Hundred-Year Flood." Of course, it began simply. It seemed to be more of the same, that usual drenching over the effluvial plain-turned-delta that constitutes most of the land we know as Bangladesh.

The river was already rising, and threatening to rise some more, that morning when Schmata's husband crossed it to go to a nearby village to pick up some food supplies. Schmata would never see him again. Friends would later say that he left early to come back, concerned about the volume of water now washing down from two of the world's greatest rivers. He apparently tried to reford what had become a raging river, and his body was never found.

That night Schmata carried her two-year-old to the river's edge as she waited fearfully for her husband's return. The four-year-old, innocent and carefree, ran ahead and stood perilously close to the edge of this now great mass of murky brown water.

The ground was soft, the bank already eroded underneath,

and in a tragedy that would be repeated thousands of times in the next few days, the tenuous land mass gave way to the onrushing waters, and a little life was snatched away.

Schmata watched, horrified as the child's head bobbed twice to the surface. She could almost reach her. She could perhaps retrieve her if she threw herself into the water, but she was carrying the two-year-old. That made her hesitate just long enough for that opportunity of a moment to pass.

We talk about the "poorest of the poor." How are they defined? They are defined by Schmata's predicament. She was forced to choose, not from a position of strength but from a position of abject weakness. Does she jeopardize one child in an attempt to rescue another? She was forced to make a decision, again, not from strength but from weakness. And the magnitude of the decision thrust upon her precludes ethical considerations. "Options that preclude ethical considerations; limited options based on impossible choices"—that's poverty! And poverty has a face; it's the face of Schmata.

And the story is not yet over. For the next three days, Schmata's grief was upstaged by her own need for survival. Food was gone. The water was polluted. Help was cut off. Unbeknownst to Schmata, the tube well in her village was underwater and already contaminated. Diarrhea attacked the fragile system of her remaining child, and within three days, Schmata was all alone.

Again, the names are fictional, but they are presented in the real context of the thousands of people, mostly children, who lost their lives in this calamity. I give them names to make sure that poverty has a face.

Poverty does have a face. And environmentally induced poverty also has a face. Sometimes it's the same face. You see, we already know what's wrong. We would all probably agree that we have environmental problems. We just haven't put a face—a human face—on the impact of those problems.

The problem is environmental degradation. It wasn't discussed prior to the flood, but global warming may have accelerated the glacier melt high in the Himalayas. That, plus harder than normal rains, brought unexpectedly large volumes of water crashing down the mountainsides.

Unfortunately, many of those mountainsides had already been denuded by massive deforestation. Commercial interests fueled by greed, and poor individuals who desperately needed a cheap energy resource, had collectively stripped the mountains, slashed and burned the hillsides, until there was nothing to hold back the high volume of water that was cascading down.

The topsoil also came down. The most productive soil on the mountainside ended up in one of three rivers: the Indus, the Ganges, or the Brahmaputra. Carried along by the force of the water, ultimately deposited in this large delta area of Bangladesh, fifteen million tons of sediment a year provides a giant clog in the natural drainage system of Bangladesh.

The drain clogs, the waters rise. Rotting carcasses, human and animal alike, contaminate the water. Insects multiply. Personal human hygiene is a joke. Epidemics run wild. The numbers of dead and dying mount. They can't be buried. Their bodies are strapped to rafts made of banana trees until the water recedes.

Perhaps the water, the focus of this tragedy, could have been siphoned off upstream in other countries, but the concept of interdependence is new. Upstream embankments have been built, and the water all stayed within the river banks—until it reached Bangladesh.

I paddled through the streets of Dhaka, observing the chaos. And yes, as the apostle Paul says, all creation was groaning (Romans 8:22). "The earth is the LORD's" (Psalm 24:1), but as you look at the environmental basket case that is Bangladesh today, we are tempted to add, "and he can have it!"

Folks, when bad things happen, the poor are normally impacted first. And when bad things happen to poor people, it is the children who absorb the most devastating impact. Let me be very specific. A degraded environment is a stumbling block to kids. And Jesus had his harshest words for anyone who would put a stumbling block in front of a child. "It would be better if a millstone were put around his neck and he would go and jump into the lake" (see Matthew 18:6). Jesus obviously knew: if the millstone wouldn't get him, the polluted, undrinkable, silted water would probably do the sucker in!

The floods of Bangladesh are stumbling blocks for children. And they are not the only stumbling blocks for children. Five years after the disaster at Chernobyl, a disaster caused by human ineptitude, it is the children who populate the hospitals. The destruction of Bhopal, a product of human negligence, was largely visited upon those who were least likely to do anything about it, namely the children. And today, if you would go to the Guatemala City dump—and there are people in this room who have been to that dump with me—if you would go to the dump, you would see a workforce composed almost entirely of children. We called the dump Gehenna, "Hell on earth." Hell, where "the fire is not quenched"—the internal combustion, the spontaneous combustion of refuse has its own perpetuity. Hell, where the "worm does not die" (Mark 9:48). In that great dump, maggots are the only thing more ubiquitous than the kids. Maggots and kids: in terms of sanctity of life, a human meltdown. Noxious fumes, polluted refuse, contaminated lives. As one of our member said, "The kids were in the dump, and the dump was in them."

And all of this, unfortunately, is still being played out before us today. But the tendency of the Christian—and especially the evangelical Christian, which I am— is to look toward the future. We almost sang this song today, "The earth is not my home, I'm just a passing through." It's a nice song. I sang it many times when I was growing up. It's a song of hope and a song of great spiritual truths. We do believe that the Kingdom is coming. But as a stand-alone concept, as a single-minded hope, as a moral imperative that exists only in a future time, this song proclaims lousy theology!

Jesus Christ, the one whose return we await, is also the one who said, "The kingdom of heaven *is* near" (Matthew 4:17). Jesus, who has already come, represents, as King, the beginning of the Kingdom that we are to "seek *first*" (Matthew 6:33). And

God announces this Kingdom in Isaiah 61:1: "The LORD has anointed me to preach good news [salvation] to the poor."

So the mustard seed of the Kingdom has been planted. The full flowering of that tree is yet to come. But the question that absolutely must dominate our minds today as Christians who want to exert leadership in this world is simply this: What do we do until he comes? What do we do today until he returns? Or, as Francis Schaeffer poetically said (and I think he got this from Ezekiel, but Schaeffer was an early environmentalist, so we'll let him plagiarize at least once in his life), "How should we then live?"

Walter Brueggeman, an Old Testament scholar, refers to Moses' role in the Exodus with a beautiful phrase, "leadership between oases"—leadership between the luxurious Egyptian fleshpots and the land of great promise. The New Testament equivalent of that image, I believe, is "leadership between kingdoms," between the one ushered in by our incarnate God two thousand years ago, and the consummation of that Kingdom upon his return. And between these two kingdoms, the most important question is, What do we do, what leadership do we bring, until he returns?

We've heard a lot of biblical thought and biblical verse, but I have a couple more to add. The first one is fairly general, and the second is more specific. Let me read a very familiar passage, Genesis 1:1-2: "In the beginning God created the heavens and earth. Now the earth was formless and empty, darkness was over the surface of the deep, and the Spirit of God was hovering over the waters." Familiar?

God is clearly Creator of our environment, but interestingly the earth "was formless and empty, with darkness over the surface of the deep." There is a Hebrew expression for this, *tohu wabohu*. But you know, sometimes that word is used in Scripture to talk about chaos, formlessness, and void, in association with darkness, water, and sea, and sometimes it refers to something or someone who is under judgment. Now you may not be inclined to believe me, but that is because you have not heard this interpretation. However, I encourage you to check it out yourself. Using a concordance, start with Jeremiah 4:23-26, and you will begin a fascinating study.

Now we can wrestle with the "why" of judgment (if you believe there is a judgment), but regardless of our answer, we see God's answer in the rest of Genesis 1. God transcends the formlessness, the void, the chaos and creates a cosmos, a world, a perfect fulfillment of his divine will.

Please recognize this for what it is: the first indication of the salvation theme, the first indication of the redemption theme. Salvation, which will dominate the first twelve chapters of Genesis, and indeed all of Scripture, comes to us in the first chapter, in the second verse of the Bible, as we begin the creation narrative.

Hold that thought while we look more specifically at what has become "The World Vision Psalm," Psalm 146. I'm just going to read verses five through nine.

Blessed is he whose help is the God of Jacob,
   whose hope is in the LORD his God,
   the Maker of heaven and earth,
   the sea, and everything in them—
   the LORD who remains faithful forever.
He upholds the cause of the oppressed
   and gives food to the hungry.
The LORD sets prisoners free,
   the LORD gives sight to the blind,
   the LORD lifts up those who are bowed down,
   the LORD loves the righteous.
The LORD watches over the alien
   and sustains the fatherless and the widow.

A quick summary of this psalm might read, "Blessed hope comes from the Creator." Indeed, from whom else could it come? And, if creation is in the all-powerful hands of our God, certainly salvation, our ultimate hope, is there, as well. In the meantime, he is the only one who can sustain faith; he "keeps faith forever"—a divine sustainable development! But listen to the bulk of the passage: He executes justice for the oppressed; gives food to the hungry; sets the prisoner free; opens the eyes of the blind; raises up this and that. Who is this God? Who is this Creator? Who is this one who orders cosmos out of chaos? He's the one who cares for the poor, the dispossessed, the marginalized, the oppressed, the vulnerable.

Folks, our Lord and Savior put a human face on poverty long before we did. And his concern for the degradation of creation is inextricably linked to his concern for those whose options for life have been severely degraded as well. The poor!

Why would Christians care about the environment? Because left unattended, the environment becomes a poverty issue. And the God we worship, the one who created order out of chaos, the one who provided salvation, cares for the poor.

So what do we do until he comes? What leadership do we bring? I think we do what he would have done. The psalmist suggests that we engage the Creator through hope. Perhaps we need to be signs of hope. Signs of hope are also signs of the Kingdom. We are kingdom people. We are leaders between kingdoms. Christian leadership needs to demonstrate, to *be* a witness of hope—hope in a chaotic world. Christians do need to lead between kingdoms, the kingdom at hand, and the kingdom of our coming Lord! We do that by honoring the God of creation—today. And in Bangladesh we do that by honoring the "least of his creatures," the children, the vulnerable, those who need care in the slums and in the villages. We do that by providing effective stewardship of that creation—today.

In Bangladesh, the Potable Water Project is a practical example of effective stewardship of creation at a grassroots level. We do that by taking a special interest in the poor—today. In Bangladesh, we do that by empowering the poor, by teaching them small enterprise development. We do that by removing stumbling blocks from children—today. We have three child survival projects providing health care for over two hundred thousand children in Bangladesh. We do that by providing hope in the midst of despair.

Let me return to the Bangladesh flood and a sign of that hope.

This hundred-year flood affected everybody. World Vision had a staff of 125 in Bangladesh. Seventy-five of our staff had their homes completely inundated and destroyed by water. Part of an involvement with the poor is a solidarity with them, and when the environment is degraded, either directly or indirectly, we are allowed to feel the same kinds of pain. The staff put its own problems aside. They had been working day and night to help those who needed help and who were most vulnerable. The day before, we discovered sixty-five thousand people stranded on a narrow levy of land, about twenty feet wide and fifty miles long. They did not have food; they hadn't had food for three days. On this day, we would take a large barge of food down to them.

The staff began loading the barge at about 3:00 A.M. When I got there about 6:00 A.M., the job was almost done. Our field director, John Key, was standing in the back of the barge with a huge smile on his face, leading his tired, preoccupied staff in song: "This is the day that the Lord has made; we will rejoice and be glad in it."

Over and over, these tired folks, these distraught people, these people who were thinking about their families and their homes and everything else, were singing; they were clapping their hands; they were lifting up their hearts; they were witnessing to the hope that was within them.

Yes, there *is* hope. The future *is* bright. It's going to get better! The Christian can look forward to a future full of unimaginable opportunities. And, yes, it's even okay to long for that day! But *this day*, today, is also the *day* that the Lord hath made.

Christians understand passion and urgency. We also know that the day of grace is not forever. What can we do *today* that will allow us to "rejoice and be glad"? What can we do today that will demonstrate that the Kingdom is indeed being sought first? We can honor our Lord and our Creator, our Savior and our Friend, by bearing witness to his grace and restoring his creation in such a way that human dignity is more possible for those who are, this day, most vulnerable.

[This sermon was delivered to the Washington Forum on May 2, 1995.]

Part Four

We Aren't "into Nature"—What about the City and Its Problems?

For many, environmentalism is the concern of the wealthy who fish for trout and want clean water in their streams. Others think that suburban bird-watchers are the ones best equipped to handle ecological concerns. Perhaps most environmentalists are people who enjoy hiking and camping. At any rate, many city dwellers feel that "the environment" is a peripheral issue compared to the many pressing concerns of the urban world.

However, thinking biblically, we must affirm that the *entire* planet belongs to the Creator (Psalm 24:1). Every molecule is creation. Every inch is owned by the Maker. We are all created and live within creation. We understand that God created both people and pigeons. God even identifies himself as the Maker of the poor (Proverbs 14:31), the Maker of both mountains *and* minorities. Suburbanite and slum dweller breathe the same air. The fishing stream in the country eventually flows into the city. Indeed, we cannot draw lines dividing creation into "theirs" and "ours." Creation is *all* God's, and his command is for all people to "take care of" the garden (Genesis 2:15).

These sermons provide an invaluable service by portraying creation care as a viable, even vital, calling for inner city ministries. Earth keeping is a valid ministry for *all* God's people, no matter where they are serving.

God's Holy Presence in a Pagan World. Some of the best sermons are those that tell a story that provides an example and challenges to action. In this sermon, J. Alfred Smith Sr. tells us about Christians in Oakland, California, who are actively caring for creation in the inner city. Smith "gives us a witness" and calls us to tend the Garden in the city.

Somebody's Knocking at Your Door. Dean Trulear serves in a city that is experiencing urban decline. Trulear says about his sermon: "What we suffer in Paterson is directly related to the historic attempts of humankind to control creation with the maximization of profits and productivity as the primary end. This sermon is an effort to call for a response to our current situation, i.e., a city which lives as an afterthought of failed attempts to harness creation, and how the stewardship of creation can help us reclaim the city as a place in harmony with creation as depicted in the book of Revelation." Trulear hears Jesus knocking on the door of his church. Perhaps you, too, will hear the knock!

God's Holy Presence in a Pagan World

J. Alfred Smith Sr.

This is how you should pray:
"Our Father in heaven,
hallowed be your name,
your kingdom come,
your will be done
     on earth as it is in heaven.
Give us today our daily bread."
          —Matthew 6:9-11

Introduction

Where is God in the world? Is the holy presence of God active in a profane world? Why should God be the concern of practical-minded people who measure life in terms of secular criteria? Does not the idea of God "turn off" common, everyday persons whose daily struggle is not about what God can do for them but what they can do for themselves? Does not the secular mind order life according to the rules of science, math, economics, and politics? Don't many learned people believe that faith has no place in a world governed by logic and scientific evidence?

Nevertheless, a loss of confidence now challenges faith in the secular gods of human accomplishment and self-sufficiency. The secular gods of technology and scientific discovery are powerless to control human greed. The ethics of self-interest and human mania for power are out of control. Humankind destroys the weakest and the impoverished in human societies and is fast moving beyond genocide to ecocide. The destruction of the environment is the ultimate destruction that shuts the open door of the future, with all of its possibilities and potential. What is needed in our postmodern world is to change the price tags we have placed on creation. New price tags will indicate that human beings, animals, and the environment are precious because they are created by God; they are sacred. Their sacredness does not require that we become pantheists who worship creation and its creatures as gods; their sacredness *does* require that all creation be respected, and that it not be exploited to bring money and wealth to any powerful interest group. God, the Creator, who is holy, gave the creation this sacred quality as a divine expression of love and grace. Therefore, the prayer "Hallowed be your name" is a plea for the sanctifying presence of God. It serves as a reminder to humans, who have drained creation of its dignity.

Making Holy the Inner City

Many secular conservation groups now fight to save the whales and animal life from extinction. They fight to clean up rivers and lakes. They are to be commended for their efforts to preserve creation and its balance. Sadly, some Bible-believing preachers have given up on honoring God's creation. They fail to see how the creation can promote an inner discipline of tranquility in a stressful society. They point to an ecologically sterilized city that they call "heaven" and that will exist in their version of the "new creation." Their listeners embrace this preaching by placing bumper stickers on their automobiles that say "Beam Me Up" or "When the Rapture Occurs This Automobile Will Be without a Driver."

A mature Christian response is not an escapist one that either withdraws or runs away from ecological evils. A mature Christian response that demonstrates God's holy presence in the inner city is taking place in Oakland, California. In the community of East Oakland where I serve, a beautiful park was developed for poor, inner-city children and adults. It was named after a well-loved African American educator who inspired teachers and pupils to work harmoniously for academic excellence. His name is Verdese Carter. For three years, many of us enjoyed the park, but then toxic waste seeped to the surface. Alert citizens organized, with the help of progressive-minded churches, to pressure city government to find the money to make the park safe from the toxic waste left by an irresponsible factory. This industry had deserted the city when poor African Americans and Hispanics moved into the neighborhood to live with older whites who were unable to move to suburbia.

It is not enough to preach about living responsible Christian lives. Those who stop with mere words unknowingly rob the name of God of its distinctive majesty. They promote the idea that a holy God is far too distant to enter into the ugly ghetto of the inner city to adorn it with hope, health, wholeness, and happiness.

Since God is not an absentee landlord, as the deists have argued with their naturalistic world-view, the Allen Temple Baptist Church Development Corporation decided to remove ugly eyesores that degrade morals and devalue property in the inner city. At Eighty-second Avenue and East Fourteenth Street, they purchased an ugly dumping ground for wrecked automobiles. With assistance from Housing and Urban Development, an attractive housing complex for seniors stands as an inner city microcosm of the garden of Eden. This beautifully landscaped housing complex with well-manicured lawns provides homes for the elderly and hallows the name of God.

In response to the unsightly, boarded-up building on the corner of East Fourteenth Street and Seventy-sixth Avenue, Allen Temple Christians, with the help of HUD, are now building twenty-five apartments to provide homes for people who are HIV positive or who have AIDS. This is the first effort of an African American church in America to clean up a neighborhood while bringing health and hope to people with AIDS, many of whom are rejected by family and treated as lepers by society. While middle-class and well-to-do Sierra Club members in the almost exclusively white suburbs of California fight powerful land developers and government interests in order to protect nature from exploitation, humble, working-class African Americans practice theological reflection and action to unveil God's holy presence in the deserted neighborhoods of the inner city. God's holy presence is a real presence, purging, purifying, and preserving the handiwork of creation.

The neglected inner city is part of creation, just as mountains and beaches are. God loves the city as he does any part of creation. Christians, therefore, must work beyond the campuses of local churches to hallow the name of God wherever they serve. They must make sure that they are the incarnation of Jesus Christ as their human hands work with God to sanctify profane environments.

The Process for Making Holy the Inner City

Planning, preparation, prayer, and perspiration are important for producing constructive change. A body of Christians who present themselves as the visible body of the invisible Christ will challenge the powers and principalities that preserve the status quo. But at times, introverted congregations preoccupied with institutional maintenance fail to respond to the cries of helpless children and demoralized adults. When this happens, the purposes of God are not defeated. From outside organized expressions of Christianity, God must often work to purge environments of ecological evil. In 1981, Chappell Hayes and Nancy Nadel moved into West Oakland with a deep sense of justice and righteous indignation. They stopped a chemical company on Thirty-second Street from spilling hazardous chemicals in the street where children were playing. Together, these two people succeeded in getting the Port of Oakland to pass an ordinance stopping the shipment of spent nuclear fuel rods through West Oakland, where the working classes live. When Chappell Hayes died, I was asked to preside at his memorial service. Clergy from the Catholic, Protestant, and Jewish communities assisted me. People of all races attended the funeral.

Now Nancy Nadel was left alone to fight the good fight of

righteousness. Ms. Nadel learned that the local water district wanted to build a huge storm water basin within fifty feet of her neighbors' houses. The basin would have been the size of two football fields and would have been filled, at times of heavy rains, with raw sewage and massive amounts of toxic chlorine. After much community organizing, the project was stopped and the water district placed the basin on the site of the sewage treatment plant itself, which is located far from residents. Nancy Nadel even became the first woman president of the water district, after winning the struggle for ecological justice.

The struggle continues. Freeways continue to be built in minority communities and in the communities of the poor. The emissions of large diesel trucks cause cancer. People who live near these freeways are often ill from air pollution. Liquor stores find it easy to get permits in poor communities. Almost every corner in the inner city has a store that sells liquor. Drug sales also take place in front of the liquor stores. Clean air, clean sidewalks and streets, and clean businesses that constitute clean environments come to pass only when the name of God is hallowed.

> May God's holy presence enter into our thinking and into our living. May the ecology of our souls be sane, and may the sacred presence of God in our character manifest itself in our daily walk and work. May the places where we live and work cease to be fallen manifestations of paradise lost. May nature join hands with all living creatures in joyous celebration of paradise regained. May we follow Jesus Christ, our paradigm, in hallowing the name of God in whatever place God calls us to live and serve. Amen.

If this transforming prayer is answered in our lives, then as Reinhold Niebuhr has said, "Our children's children will not inherit an ash-heap."

Somebody's Knocking at Your Door

Harold Dean Trulear

To the angel of the church in Laodicea write:

These are the words of the Amen, the faithful and true witness, the ruler of God's creation. I know your deeds, that you are neither cold nor hot. I wish you were either one or the other! So, because you are lukewarm— neither hot nor cold—I am about to spit you out of my mouth. You say, "I am rich; I have acquired wealth and do not need a thing." But you do not realize that you are wretched, pitiful, poor, blind and naked. I counsel you to buy from me gold refined in the fire, so you can become rich; and white clothes to wear, so you can cover your shameful nakedness; and salve to put on your eyes, so you can see. Those whom I love I rebuke and discipline. So be earnest, and repent. Here I am! I stand at the door and knock. If anyone hears my voice and opens the door, I will come in and eat with him, and he with me. To him who overcomes, I will give the right to sit with me on my throne, just as I overcame and sat down with my Father on his throne. He who has an ear, let him hear what the Spirit says to the churches.
—Revelation 3:14-22

Then the angel showed me the river of the water of life, as clear as crystal, flowing from the throne of God and of the Lamb down the middle of the great street of the city. On each side of the river stood the tree of life, bearing twelve crops of fruit, yielding its fruit every month. And the leaves of the tree are for the healing of the nations. No longer will there be any curse. The throne of God and of the Lamb will be in the city, and his servants will serve him. They will see his face, and his name will be on their foreheads. There will be no more night. They will not need the light of a lamp or the light of the sun, for the Lord God will give them light. And they will reign for ever and ever. The angel said to me, "These words are trustworthy and true. The Lord, the God of the spirits of the prophets, sent his angel to show his servants the things that must soon take place." "Behold, I am coming soon! Blessed is he who keeps the words of the prophecy in this book."

—Revelation 22:1-7

The book of Revelation is like blood in the water to the sharks of biblical prophecy. So many approach its pages for insight and direction with respect to issues of the future, the end times, and the second coming of Christ. Beasts and angels, seas of glass and lakes of fire, a veritable feast of images is served up to us as meaningful symbols concerning what *will* happen to humanity and the world in which we live. Charts, books, and graphs parade across the horizons of the prophetic sky like North Stars assuring us of the truth of some well-intentioned interpreter's vision for the future.

And yet, such futuristic interpretations often overlook the present, especially the present as addressed by John from the Isle of Patmos. For these words were originally addressed to Christians who were concerned with the present—a present fraught with turmoil and trial, persecution and oppression. Suspend judgment on the future lake of fire for a moment; John's sermon was preached to Christians *under* fire.

The emperor Domitian had put grave pressures on the young Christian church. Rome loomed large in the minds of contemporary believers, for its emperor and its empire had turned up the heat on anyone who dared to believe that Domitian was not god and his empire not the kingdom. "Worldliness," so often reduced to violations of personal piety in modern definitions, presented itself as a system where the good of the empire was the goal and the worship of the emperor was the norm. People who defied Domitian were in trouble. Death, imprisonment, exile, and torture became the fate of those exposed as opponents of "Domitianity." How should Christians respond?

Indeed, how should they have responded to a regime in which the ways of society and the worship of humanity were the order of the day? How should they have responded to a regime in which political exploitation and economic oppression were dominant motifs in the public ethic? How should they have responded when love, justice, and care for the world were replaced by division, domination, and the triumph of human ingenuity to master resources in the world at large?

John writes as one who would not compromise; indeed, exile on Patmos was punishment for his intentional noncooperation with the Roman emperor. John writes to those who struggle with compromise; indeed, seven churches in the heat of struggle with Domitian's reign are identified as recipients of his message of encouragement, warning, and inspiration. With the press of the world all around them, they struggled to be faithful to Christ. One church is praised for its effort but rebuked for losing its first love. Another is admonished to hold on under increasing persecution. Still another is told that its reputation for being alive masks the truth of its emptiness and death. Two churches are given the word that they are majoring in profession while minoring in action. They could "talk the talk" but didn't "walk the walk." One church is singled out for its true faithfulness and is promised an "open door that no man can shut."

But the last church on the list offers a curious case, an interesting challenge. The last church on the list, the church at Laodicea, arrests our attention today by virtue of its familiarity; it has a ring to it—I declare, I've seen it somewhere before.

This church, caught in the tension between Domitian and Christ, was a victim of the tug-of-war between Rome and Jerusalem. Pulled back and forth by the conflicting pressures of heaven and earth, this church is located in a setting that jars my memory, maybe like Yogi Berra's "déjà vu all over again."

This church is located in a city known for its textile industry. Clothing, fine clothing, raiment designed to communicate worth and status—this was manufactured in Laodicea.

I know a city like that.

This church is located in a city with a key role in the economic order of the region. Banking and finance brought many to the city's doors as Laodicea established itself as a trade center and city of economic opportunity.

I know a city like that.

This church is located in a city with a famous hospital, or better put, an institution of healing. It was a specialty hospital, giving particular attention to the eyes.

I know a city like that.

This was a city whose role in the economy offered the historic temptation to lose sight (pun intended; God offers it in the text) of the true source of all resources. This was a city of textiles and gold, hospitals, doctors and spas, all representative of the human spirit and its ability to master the world around it, to use resources for its own benefit, and to place the common good behind individual prosperity and wealth. "Domitianity" was alive and well in Laodicea. But I still feel this haunting sense of the familiar.

Wait a minute—I recognize the tune. Hold on, I know this song. Yes, that's it—it's the familiar refrain often repeated on the banks of our own river, the Passaic. This same melody is sung right here in Paterson, New Jersey. This song was composed in 1792, when myth has it that George Washington and Alexander Hamilton were having a picnic, not too far from here. They heard a roaring sound and went to investigate. Through the trees, they could see a mist. But, oh, when they came to a clearing, they saw the source of this dramatic sound, what we now call the Great Falls of the Passaic, that majestic waterfall that called our city into being.

Hamilton had been ambassador to France and had seen the great French industrial city, Lyons. Paris was the city of lights, but Lyons was the economic generator. Paris was the city of romance, but it was financed by Lyons. Lady Love dwelt by the Seine, but Dame Fortune worked at Lyons's burgeoning factories. And Hamilton suggested that a "Lyons of the United States" could be built right there in New Jersey, harnessing the power of the falls. Ingenious, creative, human industry at its zenith—a city where the maximization of creation's resources would spur economic growth.

They then needed to convince the skeptical governor of New Jersey, but Governor William Paterson bought into the plan for obvious reasons. The familiar tune had been composed. Our city, our American Laodicea, was born.

Textiles dominated our early industry. If you bought fine raiment of silk in the nineteenth century, chances were that it came from Paterson, the "Silk City." The mill runs from the Great Falls powered many a factory. Proximity to New York accelerated our role as a major player in world economics. The locomotive industry was based here. So was Samuel Colt's firearm manufacturing. There was a time when "Colt 45" in Paterson meant bullets, not beer. Oh, and check the national reputation of St. Joseph's Hospital. It's on the map; many of us who migrated here from the South came to work there. Laodicea, one more time—"déjà vu all over again."

And the church was here—the church *is* here—*still* struggling with Domitianity. Paterson made a historic choice to trust in the might of its industry rather than the almighty one. Paterson made a clear choice to compromise with the dominant economic ethos, rather than to hold out for the New Jerusalem. Paterson decided, and the churches complied, that its well-being would rest in its ability to harness creation, rather than to be in harmony with it; to control it, rather than to care for it. Management canceled out stewardship; the environment became the handmaid of industrial progress, all fueled by the wonders of a waterfall.

People who looked like you and me, indeed, many of us here, came to Laodicea—I mean Paterson—precisely because it offered the economic opportunity afforded by such an ethic of progress. Uncritical of this ethic, and genuinely and authentically desirous of the economic security it provided, we came—an African American labor force to keep Laodicea going.

But trust in that order breeds dependence on that order—look where it has gotten us. The factories are gone. Colt 45s are replaced by automatic weapons. Silk is imported. Warehouses are abandoned. The jobs we came for have moved to other parts of the world, or simply disappeared.

Now, in fairness, I don't know how many churches would have seen this coming. After all, Domitian's ethics, Babylonian images of prosperity, have so permeated the church that it would be hard to see. But the results are not. And whether we have been owners, reaping the benefits of the harnessing of creation, or we came to Laodicea uncritical of its politics of control but grateful for its promise of employment, there is a word from the Lord for us. Wealthy and poor Christians, both trusting in the same system, must hear these words: "I know your deeds, that you are neither cold nor hot. I wish that you were either one or the other!" (Revelation 3:15).

No, we are not cold, indifferent to the reality of the one who is "the Amen, the faithful and true witness, the ruler of God's creation." We gather to praise his name every Sunday; we lift our hands heavenward on a regular basis; we assemble each Lord's day morning to hear, "Thus saith the Lord."

But neither are we hot. The temperature of our worship seems to measure high, but the "ice" of cooperation and integration with the status quo has been thrown into the "hot spring" of ecstatic worship and rendered our testimony lukewarm. We are lukewarm Christians in the mouth of a nauseated God, in a sense rightfully happy to be gainfully employed in the city and yet blind to the mess left for us by this system's manipulation of creatures and creation.

When God calls to the church at Laodicea, he rebukes the people for trusting in the system by using images for repentance that point to the very industries in which they had laid faith. The textile city that manufactures clothing is "naked." The mecca where people came for the healing of the eyes is "blind." This metropolis of thriving commerce is "poor."

I don't think that it is very hard for us to see the poverty, sickness, and destitution in our modern Laodicea. I don't think it would be very difficult for us to admit that we have placed more confidence in Domitian's reign than we ought. It may very well be that Paterson today, indeed much of urban America, bears the marks of misplaced trust in Domitian. For when Domitian moves the factories, when Domitian goes global in international interest, when Domitian decides that suburbs, interstates, air travel, and nuclear weapons will replace city neighborhoods, public transportation, and local industry, then we see the folly of cooperating with the emperor. Trash piles up in the streets as dwindling tax bases accelerate the decline of city services. The factories leave behind toxic waste in cities like nearby Jersey City, where Monumental Baptist Church and Pastor Willard Ashley have waged a noble struggle that has attracted international attention. Bus depots that no one wants in their backyard belch diesel emissions that cloud above the heads of children going to School 13, Dawn Treader Elementary, and our own Paterson community schools. Domitian still runs the city; he just doesn't live here anymore. The city was once the site of the exploitation of the area resources, but now it is seen as the receptacle of area trash.

But there's a sound I hear. Above the din of Interstate 80's trucks roaring above our heads—I hear a sound. Above the noise of buses starting their engines on Madison Avenue—I hear a sound. Piercing screams of a child who has cut her foot on a broken bottle in a vacant lot cannot drown out this sound. The whirring hum of contractor's equipment in the business of asbestos removal in school buildings is not an effective muffler. This sound cannot be hid. It is not stealthy, like toxic waste left behind to do its work.

I hear a sound.

It is a knock. Do you hear it? It is a knock—sure and steady. There is a knock; yes, *there's somebody knocking at our door!*

Jesus is knocking. He has not given up on Laodicea. Jesus is knocking. There is hope for Laodicea. Jesus is knocking. The ultimate destiny of Laodicean saints is still in view. Jesus is knocking, and he has a word for us in Paterson today.

He says, "If anyone hears my voice . . ."

Oh, I am glad he said "anyone." That's equal opportunity that can't be dismissed by our legislators. He said "anyone." That's egalitarian ethics at its highest. "Anyone"—that's a democratic call that critiques Domitian's claim to a corner on the information market.

I am so glad Jesus didn't say, "If the politicians hear . . ."

I am so glad he didn't say, "If the factory owners hear . . ."

I am particularly pleased he didn't say, "If the rich and powerful hear . . ."

No, this is a call to all of us who name the name of Jesus. The future of Laodicea and its churches does not rest on the decisions of its ruling class. God calls out to us for a partnership, the qualifications for which are found under the heading of "anyone": anyone who "hears my voice and opens the door!"

And if we open the door to our hearts and let him into those seats of trust still warm with the impression of Domitian's comfortable presence . . . If we let him into those closed-off areas where we hid our trust in the system's gains . . . If we let him into those backyard gardens where we nurtured ideas of economic security and tossed prophetic principles of compassion and justice into our personal landfills . . . If we let him into the dumps of our toxic, theological waste . . . If we open the door to our hearts, he promises to come in.

He promises not just to come in but to have supper. The man, woman, boy, or girl who opens his or her heart to Christ and chooses to follow him and resist the system's evil has the promise of supper with the Savior. Now, supper is a special meal. No fast-food fellowship with some wrappers and cups to dispose of quickly. He's not a drive-thru divinity. No, this supper is like that old-fashioned tradition—you remember down South—when everybody gathered around the table: no TV or radio interrupted the conversation; the day's events were rehearsed; thanks were rendered for the day's gifts, grace, and labor; and a time of family intimacy and fellowship became the ritual of belonging for everybody present. This holy ritual prepared the family for the press of the coming days.

That is what Jesus wants with you and me—a time of intimacy and fellowship, where we can talk about the issues of the day; give thanks for gifts, grace, and labor; make plans for the coming hours. He's knocking because he's looking for somebody to reject Domitian's offer of a diet of compliance and cooperation and to choose the fullness of the feast at his feet.

He's knocking today. His knock says, "I have not given up on Paterson." It says, "I still have hope for the city." It says, "There is opportunity for your renewal, if you let me in." It declares, "I am looking for people of faith who will turn toward me and away from Domitian, turn toward the new Jerusalem and away from Rome, turn to new life and away from death. There's a reason your city looks the way it does: your trust has been in the wrong places, your heart has been wooed by the wrong song, your gaze has been fixed on the wrong source. Look to me and live."

That's what the knocking is about. It is the knock of somebody who sees our plight, receives our repentance, and offers his presence. After all, he's not an anti-urban God. He is not the Savior of suburbia only, but of the whole world. For when he makes his final move, it is to a city—not one that harnesses creation's power, but one that is in harmony with creation. That future city doesn't take its waterfall and use it to create wealth, but it does have a river, flowing clear as crystal. There are no locomotive or gun factories, but there is a tree whose fruit produces healing for the nations. There are no silk or textile mills, but somehow the bride is still dressed beautifully for her husband. He's still knocking, with invitations to this great wedding.

He knocks in part to be sure, but he knocks in response to the prayer composed by Frank Mason North many years ago, as he saw how Domitian's domain left the city in trouble. These words have echoed from urban sanctuaries across this century. He knocks because somebody prayed:

O Master from the mountainside,
Make haste to heal these hearts of pain;
Among these restless throngs abide;
O tread the city's streets again,
Till all the world shall learn your love
And follow where your feet have trod,
Till, glorious from your heaven above,
Shall come the city of our God!

[This sermon was preached at the Community Baptist Church of Love, Paterson, New Jersey, on Sunday, September 23, 1995.]

Part Five

Isn't the Environment Just One More Crisis among Many?

Martin Luther, the theologian of the Reformation, was once asked what he would do if he knew that the world would end tomorrow. His response: "Plant a tree today."

It is an amazing concept. As human history nears its final moments, here is old Martin with his shovel digging a hole for a spindly sapling.

What would *you* do if you knew that the end of the world was imminent? Perhaps you would quickly set your priorities to determine your focus. Would you want to make sure your family was prepared? Would you want society to get its values straight, finally, in preparation for the big day? Where would "the environment" fit in your list of things to tend to before the final hour?

Perhaps the end of the world is not imminent. Even so, life in this last part of the twentieth century is quite complex. Many things vie for our attention and our commitment. Not the least of these is the environment. We feel overloaded with all the crises that weigh upon us. Is the environment just one more crisis?

You might expect a volume such as this to debate vigorously the facts of the environmental crisis. What do the scientists say? How bad off is our planet? These are significant questions.

These sermons, however, will not answer these questions. As a matter of fact, these sermons may do *exactly the opposite* by inspiring you with hope and joy. This may seem odd because environmental messages rarely invoke these emotions. Environmentalists themselves often seem to be rather dour types who seem to have forgotten how to smile.

The messages and sermons in Part Five, indeed the entire volume, are not environmental messages; they are biblical messages. As such, they *do* offer hope and joy. You see, Christians have a *real* contribution to make to environmentalism. People are tired and stressed; our world desperately needs honest hope and deep-seated joy. Christians have this hope and joy to offer, a contribution that should not be underestimated. The world is waiting to hear a good word from the pulpits of our land!

Gathering Day. Creation displays the artistry of God in vivid color and glowing luminescence. If our dark world could see a bit of this glory, it just might put our challenging times into perspective. This piece, "Gathering Day" by Karen Burton Mains, brims with joy and light. She calls us into the outdoor sanctuary to worship. She bids us listen to what messages the Creator might have for us, hidden in the fine details of creation.

Childlike Wonder at the Creation is a real treat because Virginia Patterson knows kids and she knows Christian education. In "A Childlike Wonder," we have an open door to exercising our creativity as we listen to a litany of the Creator's glories. Your congregation will not fall asleep during this sermon! They will be too busy having fun.

Prayer, Praise, and Play details a rich feast of insights on how to live as people of the transcendent God. Eugene Peterson calls us to draw near the Creator God in prayer so that we might understand what he is doing so mightily in creation. Certainly, we need deep prayer lives in our complex age. Creation can be God's school of prayer.

Of Whales and Polar Bears. In spite of all its amazing discoveries and benefits, science is woefully inadequate in voicing wonder at God's amazing creation. Yancey eloquently expresses this wonder. By following his example in our preaching and witnessing, Christians can make a refreshing contribution to an environmentalism weary of its own alarmism. A sense of wonder will also revitalize biblical worship in our society, which is addicted to gimmicks and cheap entertainment.

Gathering Day: The Fields Far West of the City

Karen Burton Mains

"And he will send his angels and gather his elect from the four winds,
   from the ends of the earth to the ends of the heavens."
      —Mark 13:27

Early one day in September 1989, I woke curiously alive. What a beautiful gathering morning! I collected baskets and buckets to fill the back of the station wagon, found gloves to protect my hands, and rummaged for clippers in the kitchen catch-all drawer. Heading off to meet friends, Lou and Mary, I kept thinking, *This day we are going to gather, and it is a perfect, wonderful fall morning.*

We met at Mary La Frenz's home outside St. Charles, Illinois. Her A-frame house is planted atop one of the few ridges of high land we have in this part of the state. Hills actually loll down and away from her deck. Lou Gallagher is joining us. Lou and Mary are artists with natural arrangements. They weave vines, dried flowers, and pods into delicate wall hangings, wreaths, swags, and baskets. Unlike those who put together paint-by-number compositions, dull duplicates from many arts and crafts booths, these two are not afraid to leave the wildness in the work. Creation's oddities are respected and integrated into their designs.

I was eager to gather with these practiced field hands, who identify the weeds by name, know where to find them, and have enough experience to know which methods are best for drying which plants. Naturalists, people with literacy in the lore of the world, wake dormant yearnings in me.

Mary's basement is neatly festooned with hanging bunches: rich colored statice, yellow yarrow. Lids are lifted from barrels to show off the heads of zinnias peeking from layers of desiccants. Dried flowers are being designed for a wedding; the bridal bouquet is made of wild quinine and wispy baby's breath, and everything is tied with yards of cream satin ribbons. Mary demonstrates the use of her glue gun, a tool new to me. Wispy strands, now cooled, thread like spider's tracings through her swags and wreaths.

Terry La Frenz has built his wife a drying shed. We walk to it down a path where moss grows, up the porch into the dark interior. Here are more wreaths in the making, more hanging bunches, more hydrangea blooms air drying, bundled sheaves of grasses. Frankly, I am envious. I covet a laboratory of my own, a studio to house my experiments in form.

We start our gathering in the restored prairies that stretch westward beyond the farthest edge of these suburbs. The day is grand: blue skies, white full clouds, the sun striking color upon all growing things. I am dressed in old jeans, field boots, and a long-sleeved shirt—anything to keep scratches from bloodying me. Lou, however, is wearing shorts, her legs and arms berry-brown, like a child golden from summer's favor. We plunge into the tall weeds and grasses, the ground crunching with each step. I begin collecting purple coneflower. Already field-dried, the petals have fallen, and the rich, burgundy-brown heads stand black against the bright light. Some centers are swollen to walnut size, topping tall on proud stems. I scroll a middle finger across the porcupine texture.

I had loved the milky quinine in Mary's basement; she knows where it grows. We follow through a tree windbreak into open pasture. The heads of creamy umbels are quickly gathered into bunches. Lou, a pro, has had the foresight to bring a package of rubber bands, and my baskets are laden with the morning's booty: amber-brown wands of common mullein; bound bergamot, the leaves fragrant and even more so when crushed; clusters of wild yarrow, now a warm golden brown. Two of my baskets are full.

The only way I can describe my feelings is to say that I am purely exultant. This is undiluted pleasure. Imagine! To have *time* to walk across the land, to feel it uneven but substantial beneath my shoes. Imagine! To have time *enough*; nothing interrupts me, no one demands my attention. Surely the nature of Christ the Creator shows forth in all these things, in this grand and perfect day. What a thought! the print of the originator is on all these pods. Dust them for identification, his fingerprints show forth!

I want to caress these growing things. I want to hold them the way a parent enfolds an infant's chubby foot in the palm of her hand and draws it tucked to the mouth to kiss. And I feel spiritually responsive, alive to all that can be read in these fields, along these paths, in these tall and unthwarted blooms. Oh, to lift my hands in praise and stand solid in the middle of this field and turn in a slow, deliberate dance of exaltation. To be as unself-consciously alive as these growing things! To be as completely who God has made me to be as they are completely what God has made them to be!

Pausing, I watch the light, its effect on the stems, on the russet lace of chawed and middle-aging leaves, on the hills (such as we Illinoisians have), on the trees staining slightly umber, rose, but mostly still green. Some kind benefactor has flung shatterings that sparkle and sing silent paeans. In her book *A Natural History of the Five Senses,* author Diane Ackerman writes, "We think of our eyes as wise seers, but all the eye does is gather light." And that is what my eye is doing. I understand this. It is gathering the spilled shards of light, light on the curled dock, its lanceolated leaves twisting and drying, its thousand beads turned a rich, red brown. I am gathering the light on the dun nodding thistle, bleached wheat-gold, flat-domed, with a velvet butter center. I am gathering light.

The light is so stunning I can understand that it is also dangerous. Intoxicating, addictive, blinding, it can interfere with a day's serious study, with solemn work. El Greco, the great painter who made his final home in Toledo, Spain, developed, like many geniuses in late age, stunning spiritual qualities in his canvases. Found working by a visitor in a darkened studio, the Greek explained that "daylight blinded the light within." Increasingly he was to paint the visions of his inner eye that became so perturbing to others. Contemporaries considered his style extravagant, and he was forgotten in the centuries following his own (the late sixteenth century). Greco's captured "light within" emerged eventually to stun art aficionados of the nineteenth century who reestablished his reputation as one of the greatest geniuses of Western art.

Light can be dangerous—the dazzling light of the exterior world with its shades and variations, and the light of the inner world, difficult to interpret and translate to the viewer. "The true light that gives light to every man was coming into the world. He was in the world, and though the world was made through him, the world did not recognize him. He came to that which was his own, but his own did not receive him" (John 1:9-11). A see-er must learn how to view the light, how to gather it, then what to do with it.

Georgia O'Keefe, the American artist, once said, "To see takes time." Indeed, most of us traverse this world seeing very little. The natural world rarely stuns us. We do not see it; we only glance at it. To see the physical world, to really observe, takes time. The world cannot be viewed well from a speeding car, though we fool ourselves into thinking that we have "seen" the mountain, the river, the prairie. To see the world, we must climb the mountain, sit beside the river, and walk in the prairie. We must see the world closely enough to learn what to call it. Then we must pause beside it to consider what it means. Frederick Turner once wrote that Thoreau learned to look "so deeply into a natural fact that at last it reveals its hidden spiritual dimension." Gathering days force me to see and to honor the beauty of what I habitually ignore or neglect.

These things are also true of seeing with the eyes of the soul. Seeing takes time. So few of us moderns know how to gaze outward or inward or upward with spiritual insight. We are blinded to the physical beauty beating around us that points toward the truths of the spiritual beauties to which we are also sightless. Somehow, there is a synergy between the two; learning to see in either of the arenas, the natural world or the spiritual world, can be a practice discipline for apprehending the other. The early church father John of Damascene once explained that "visible images are often symbols of the invisible realities, so that through the material things we gain a certain idea of the immaterial realities."

So we must become gatherers. We must learn to gather light spiritually and to take care lest it stun us beyond reason's ability to understand it. We must learn to gather the light of Christ as it reflects off other Christians. We must learn to honor them, even though their Christian forms, most often different from our own, are not quite what we desire. We must learn to understand that they shed his brilliant presence in the darkness. We must learn to gather light with a rigorous and dedicated study of theology. And rather than manipulate this manifestation of divine light to create it in our own image, we must be broken and receptive and let the light create us in the image of the one we have been framing with doctrine. We must watch the light shine from the pages of Scripture and not become arrogant in our own learning; the study is to inform and to change and to re-create us, not simply for the sake of intellectual prowess. We must catch sight of the match struck, tracking an incandescent line through the dark woods of our living by the Holy Spirit, both knowable and inscrutable. We must learn to live with the paradoxes of seeing that are like the paradoxes of the incarnation: "The one who was invisible becomes visible." Seeing takes time. It also demands humility.

Today, for me, in a rare and delicately balanced moment, the outward, material activity mates the inward, spiritual reality. I am gathering weeds, but I know that I am gathering other things as well. I am gathering time, certainly; I am gathering experiences, thoughts. But mostly I am gathering metaphorical meanings. A hundred sermons, their bare outlines forming, have also been plucked from these fields and paths. For instance, it suddenly strikes me that I am always being gathered myself (being "fetched," as Deuteronomy 30:4 describes it). "If any of thine be driven out unto the outmost parts of heaven, from thence will the LORD thy God gather thee, and from thence will he *fetch* thee: and the LORD thy God will bring thee into the land . . . and will circumcise thine heart and the heart of thy seed, to love the LORD thy God with all thine heart" (Deuteronomy 30:4-6 KJV). This is an Old Testament Scripture with broader, more applicable implications. God is the gatherer, the originator of gathering days, with a primary impulse always to be bringing us back to himself. And I have never before thought of him in this way.

Walks in the world always give me the gift of new meanings to old truths. I store this one, a damp fresh impression to be pressed between the pages of my journal later.

Mary, Lou, and I are careful not to uproot any of our treasures; there are ecological courtesies to observe. Only a fraction of the pods are plucked, leaving the meadows replete with drying wildweeds. Our plundering has a beneficial effect: rustlings shake the plants—like birds, we are scattering the seed. After lugging the stuffed baskets to the roadside, I run to the parking spot to bring round the station wagon, so we can load it with the fruits of our collecting.

Mary knows of a trail where wild grapevines choke the trees. On the way, we clip smartweed, its magenta fronds drooping and curling. The weather shifts; clouds come hoofing across the blue day, pounding it gray; the air cools, forecasting a storm.

It is early noon, and gnarled wild apple trees stand sentry beside the entrance to the prairie path. We pick small, hard fruit, stuff our pockets, bite around wormholes, and the crunch, the tang are a hearty snack, all the better for being free. The trail is wide but secluded by thick undergrowth and a canopy of high trees. We collect fallen branches of shaggy-barked oak, scrape ourselves in patches of brambles as we follow a diverging footpath into the low woods. Suddenly, I see a white glimmer in the forest half-light. "Oh, look, a puffball!" I cry. "They're edible!"

Mary laughs at me. How did I see that? I look at her: how could I miss it? It's the size of a football!

All morning I have been wondering how Lou and Mary see. How did they see that bittersweet vine—without its biennial berries? How did they know the fluffy boneset would hang dry for bouquets and arrangements? How did they distinguish the snakegrass in the stand of weeds? Mary and I talk about seeing. I've taken a course in fungi identification at a local arboretum, and my eye is sensitized to bracken ledged on a tree trunk, the filigreed lichen on the forest floor. Sighting puffballs is hardly a feat—it fairly glows in the dim woods—but, nevertheless, we all find what we have been trained to see. Gently, I twist the puffball off its base. A mushroom delicacy, washed and sliced and cooked in butter—one by itself is large enough to make an entire meal for several diners.

So, another axiom exists regarding seeing: We see what we are looking for. We will find the object of our hunt. We will discover it in the world or in our daily lives; we will find it in one another. Consequently, we must make certain that what we give ourselves to gather is worthy of the hunting and the discovering. Christ told many a hunting and gathering parable (the housewife searching for a lost coin, the Good Shepherd seeking the lost sheep, and so forth). In fact, his kingdom has much to do with hiddenness, with searching out the treasure, with arduous hunts, with exultant findings. He, and his Father (we must never forget), are the consummate gatherers. "And he will send his angels and gather his elect from the four winds, from the ends of the earth to the ends of the heavens" (Mark 13:27).

My friends and I come back to the main trail. Lou has a deep scratch on one leg. She laughs it off: "Oh, I always come back a mess from gathering." In truth, we three are a sight, sweaty and windblown with burrs and wispy debris clinging, scrapes and thornpricks, mosquito bites swelling. A soft rain begins to fall, cooling us. And we are completely happy, children again at play, treasure hunting in the world.

We find carrion vine, with its solidly packed balls of blue-black berries. Then, at last, the wild grapevine. Stretching tendrils are yanked from the high branches. Mary and Lou form circlets right away, stripping the fresh leaves by pulling the vines through the channel of their fists. I loop wreaths as well but with the leaves intact; I'm curious to see how they dry.

Toting more full baskets, we head back to the car in the soft rain, our shirts damp. In addition, we've gathered whorled milkweed, redtop grass, field aster, tickseed, tansy—all neatly bunched with Lou's rubber bands. Back at Mary's home, she serves up avocado-sprouts-and-lettuce sandwiches, the underslice of bread spread with hot mustard, the whole topped with melted Swiss cheese. "This," she promises, "when eaten at every meal, is a sure-fire way of losing weight." Mary testifies that she tried the recipe for two weeks and lost ten pounds.

I sit on a stool at the kitchen counter, loving women's conversation: trading recipes; sharing news of common acquaintances, information about our church's activities, and spiritual truths. But another part of me is wondering why I feel so energized by this gathering day. I am shot full of adrenaline. It is like discovering love, or loving, or falling in love. How long has it been since I gave myself a whole day to collect the world in my hands?

Why is it always so hard to spend time doing the things we most love to do? I can smell the crushed oils of herbs on my fingertips. I vow not to let the worthy demands upon my days—child rearing, ministry and travel, wife-ing and befriending—pull me away from all the things that most quicken my soul.

Joel, our second son, is home when I return, the station wagon stuffed. His classes in film at Columbia College in Chicago don't begin until late September. To my delight, he has been laying a plywood floor in the garage attic for me, and I am grateful. We need storage space. He laughs at my bounty (what great humor I often provide for my children) and notices right away how smug I seem. Yes, I say. I have just spent a perfect, an exquisitely perfect, day. I have been gathering.

Is this how God feels when he gathers his own—content, smug, and satisfied to have done a good work, the divine chaser home after the chase, his satchels filled with live and lovely game? How beautiful are the pictures of restoration in the prophets. And how delighted the gatherer seems about his future plans:

See, I will bring them . . .
    and gather them from the ends of the earth.
Among them will be the blind and the lame,
    expectant mothers and women in labor;
    a great throng will return.
They will come with weeping;
    they will pray as I bring them back.
I will lead them . . .
They will come and shout for joy on the heights of Zion;
    they will rejoice in the bounty of the LORD. . . .
Then maidens will dance and be glad,
    young men and old as well.
I will turn their mourning into gladness;
    I will give them comfort and joy instead of sorrow.
I will satisfy the priests with abundance,
    and my people will be filled with my bounty,"
declares the LORD.
                   —Jeremiah 31:8-9, 12-14

A picture of a perfect, exquisite gathering day!

And what despair when he gathers nothing, when the harvesting yield is depleted, when the vines are fruitless. Jesus wept when he returned empty-handed: "O Jerusalem, Jerusalem, . . . how often I have longed to gather your children together, as a hen gathers her chicks under her wings, but you were not willing!" (Luke 13:34).

Together, Joel and I disgorge the station wagon. Full from front to back, it has eaten too much. Joel unscrews broom handles from the long push brooms and hangs them as rods between the bicycle hooks in the ceiling. I tie bunches with string and pass them to him on the ladder, and he secures them upside down to the broom handles. We run out of space; some weeds can season in the baskets. The remaining bunches are strung from the runners of the open overhead garage door; it will have to stay ajar. Perhaps once the floor is laid, I can convert a quarter of the attic to my own temporary drying shed.

I make frequent trips to the back door that evening for the pure pleasure of seeing the result of my day's labor. I laugh, remembering that the whole purpose of this event was for me to collect enough materials to arrange twenty centerpieces for a luncheon at our church. Having gathered enough to last for two years and for two hundred centerpieces, I am a shamefully rich woman! And all it cost me was a day in the fields far west of the city.

A weed identification book is tucked away and dusty on a library shelf. Opening it to verify the names of my treasures, I find pressed spring flowers between the pages—squirrel corn, white trout lily, toothwort—and a date: April 26, 1978. It has been over a decade since I gave myself a whole gathering day. I wonder: Has it been that long since I took time to really see?

Later, in bed—blissful, replete, content—my mind begins to rock me to sleep by weaving analogies: if I am flushed with joy at gathering the field flowers, what a state must God be in when he "fetches" his own. Does he tread the world (sending his Spirit forth) looking for finds? Does he exclaim over each particular creation, calling out to his friends, "Oh, look, a puffball beneath the trees! Oh, wild and curling grapevines! Oh, here, apples! Taste and see!"? Does he hang us up to dry so that we will become everlasting?

More intimately, when he comes to gather me, will he gloat at the discovery and say, "You are exactly what I had in mind! Just what I needed to finish the bridal bouquet!"? And will he smile and pluck me up?

I breathe my last prayer of the day, a personal compline: *Oh God, be always gathering me. Let me ever be part of your merry restoration. Let the consolation of the festival days strike rhythm on the drum of my soul. Turn my weeping into joy. Turn my sorrows into gladness. Most of all, let me see.*

Then I looked, and lo, a white cloud, and seated on the cloud one like a son of man, with a golden crown on his head, and a sharp sickle in his hand. And another angel came out of the temple, calling with a loud voice to him who sat upon the cloud, Put in your sickle, and reap, for the hour to reap has come, for the harvest of the earth is fully ripe." So he who sat upon the cloud swung his sickle on the earth, and the earth was reaped.
—Revelation 14:14-16 (RSV)

Childlike Wonder at the Creation

Virginia Patterson

[This is a participatory sermon. Following are suggestions from Virginia Patterson on how to make this sermon more effective.—Editor]

This sermon has a threefold purpose: to help adults and children share together in childlike wonder at God's creation; to nurture a desire to care for creation as a way of worshiping God; and to intentionally include children in grades 1-6 in the worship service.

To prepare for this sermon: Develop a slide presentation to accompany the reading of Psalm 104:1-23. Use images suggested by the psalm. For example, start with pictures of the sky (sunrise; stars; billowy, fast-moving clouds; trees bending with the wind; lightning; and so forth). Then show pictures of God's handiwork on earth (rivers flowing through hills and valleys, breaking ocean waves, animals drinking from streams, birds flying and nesting, cattle grazing, farm fields or gardens, trees, mountains, the moon, animals at dusk, sunrise, and the like). Or show one picture featuring the sky and then a second picture featuring earth and water. For nature slides, check such places as libraries, museums, planetariums, and nature stores. Perhaps you can use the creative gifts of photographers in your own congregation.

Finally, prepare a special children's bulletin with an outline of the sermon and places for children to list or draw responses and write the application. Include a separate page in the bulletin for adults to write or draw responses. Be sure to have plenty of sharpened pencils! And enjoy!

It's been a renewing experience for me to prepare this sermon on childlike wonder at God's creation. I've reflected on my own wonder as a child. Having been born and raised for the first thirteen years of my life in New Mexico, I thought the world was flat and dry and vast. My father used to say you could see two days ahead in New Mexico. But I can still recall looking out across the pasture and seeing nothing until land and sky met on the distant horizon. When I, as an adult, reflect on my childhood memories of that landscape, I have distinctly lonely and desolate feelings. However, more inspiring memories fill my heart when I recall the way I felt looking up at a star-filled sky. It was during those moments that the wonder of a child captured my attention. The stars were always clear and bright and close. I felt as though I were closed in and protected by the God of creation. The nighttime sky has always been the place where I've looked for God, even before I knew about the verse that says, "The heavens declare the glory of God" (Psalm 19:1 KJV).

Both adults and children stand in open-mouthed wonder when we look at God's wonderful creation. Adults and children alike feel small in comparison to his greatness. We are in awe at his greatness.

How does this make us feel? Like sitting silently and meditating? Or like clapping and smiling? Whichever we feel, we are worshiping God. We want to praise him for the fantastic things he has done in creation!

Let's look at Psalm 104 (NRSV) and see how the psalm writer felt childlike wonder at creation and praised God. As we read through each set of verses, children—and adults, too—may write down or draw a picture of the things in creation that they appreciate most.

Psalm 104 is one of the Scripture's outstanding descriptions of the glory of the natural world. The psalm is divided into three sections. The first section in verses 1-23 is a description of God's grand creation. The second section in verses 24-30 is a meditation, and a prayer closes out the third section in verses 31-35.

The first twenty-three verses describe five aspects of creation. Listen for the wonder of a child coming through as the psalm writer tells of God's marvelous doings. Share that wonder as you look at a few slides that will accompany the reading of this inspiring psalm.

Verses 1-4 show the majesty and power of God. The psalm writer tells how our majestic God is revealed through his marvelous creation. *(Show accompanying slides as you read the following verses.)*

Bless the LORD, O my soul.
O LORD my God, you are very great.
You are clothed with honor and majesty,
    wrapped in light as with a garment.
You stretch out the heavens like a tent,
    you set the beams of your chambers on the waters,
you make the clouds your chariot,
    you ride on the wings of the wind,
you make the winds your messengers,
    fire and flame your ministers.

Which of these are things you really appreciate? On your bulletin insert, write them down or draw a picture of them. *(Allow time for response.)*

Verses 5-9 cover the creation of the sea and land. The psalm writer sees our great God controlling the powerful forces of creation to make the earth a safe and secure place. *(Show accompanying slides as you read the following verses.)*

You set the earth on its foundations,
    so that it shall never be shaken.
You cover it with the deep as with a garment;
    the waters stood above the mountains.
At your rebuke they flee;
    at the sound of your thunder they take to flight.
They rose up to the mountains, ran down to the valleys

to the place that you appointed for them.
You set a boundary that they may not pass,
    so that they might not again cover the earth.

Which of these things capture your imagination? Write them
down. Be creative and draw a picture of them. *(Allow time for
response.)*

Verses 10-13 show an abundant supply of water to support
life on the earth. The psalm writer sees our caring God
ensuring that all regions and creatures get the life-giving
water they need. *(Show accompanying slides as you read the
following verses.)*

You make springs gush forth in the valleys;
    they flow between the hills,
giving drink to every wild animal;
    the wild asses quench their thirst.
By the streams the birds of the air have their habitation;
    they sing among the branches.
From your lofty abode you water the mountains;
    the earth is satisfied with the fruit of your work.

Which of these things inspire you to praise our Creator God?
Write them down or draw a picture of them. *(Allow time for
response.)*

Verses 14-18 outline the ways God provides food, especially
for humans. The psalm writer describes our generous God, who
gives excellent food for people to delight in and gives shelter to
both people and wild animals. *(Show accompanying slides as
you read the following verses.)*

You cause the grass to grow for the cattle,
    and plants for people to use,
to bring forth food from the earth,
    and wine to gladden the human heart,
oil to make the face shine,
    and bread to strengthen the human heart.
The trees of the LORD are watered abundantly,

the cedars of Lebanon that he planted.
In them the birds build their nests;
the stork has its home in the fir trees.
The high mountains are for the wild goats;
the rocks are a refuge for the coneys.

Which of these things are you thankful for? Write them down
or use your own God-given creativity and draw a picture of
them. *(Allow time for response.)*

Verses 19-23 describe how God has set the daily and seasonal
rhythms for our life and work. The psalm writer sees our wise
God organizing life on earth into patterns and cycles. *(Show
accompanying slides as you read the following verses.)*

You have made the moon to mark the seasons;
the sun knows its time for setting.
You make darkness, and it is night,
when all the animals of the forest come creeping out.
The young lions roar for their prey,
seeking their food from God.
When the sun rises, they withdraw
and lie down in their dens.
People go out to their work
and to their labor until the evening.

Which of these are things you really appreciate? Write them
down or draw a picture of them. *(Allow time for response.)*

In these verses we see the psalm writer's great range of
thought, stretching from the immensity and versatility of the
Creator in verses 1-4 to the daily routine of a person's life in
verse 23. The psalm writer's praise of God reaches from the vast
labor and purpose of the earth's creation in verses 5-9 to the
effortless song of a bird on a treetop in verse 12.

The psalm writer expresses wonder like that of a child at
things both great and small. The awesome expanse of the deep
waters that clothe the earth in verses 6-9 is contrasted with the
restful greenery of meadows and olive groves in verses 14 and
15. The timid, elusive goats of the high hills in verse 18 are as

well known as the beasts of the forest that creep stealthily in the shadows of evening in verse 20.

In all of these things, the psalm writer rejoices in God's greatness. Verses 1-9 declare that all creation is subject to the Creator. I don't know about you, but when I see the devastation caused by floods, I take great comfort in the fact that God will not again allow the waters to cover the earth. And when we see the rainbow, it's a reminder of God's promise. All creation is under his control—floods, droughts, earthquakes.

Verses 10-23 show that all creation is ordered by the Creator and blended together to provide for the needs of his many creatures. The physical universe is divinely designed to meet the needs of animals and people, as seen in verses 10-18. These animals and humans are in turn subject to the seasonal regulations, as seen in verses 19-23. As children, we are delighted with the changing seasons, and we thrive on the predictability of night and day.

When we consider all that God has created and the orderliness of it, it's natural that we are moved to meditate on these wonders. Together, let's join the psalmist in a meditation on how this varied and mighty world is utterly dependent upon its Creator as I read verses 24-30.

O LORD, how manifold are your works!
    In wisdom you have made them all;
    the earth is full of your creatures.
Yonder is the sea, great and wide,
    creeping things innumerable are there,
    living things both small and great.
There go the ships,
    and Leviathan [the mythical sea monster] that you formed to
        sport in it.
These all look to you
    to give them their food in due season;
when you give to them, they gather it up;
    when you open your hand, they are filled with good things.
When you hide your face, they are dismayed;

when you take away their breath, they die
and return to their dust.
When you send forth your spirit, they are created;
and you renew the face of the ground.

All things have been created by the Spirit of God who continuously renews earth's natural life from year to year. Amazing! Awesome! Wonderful!

We are not surprised that the psalmist turns to God in praise as he concludes this creative masterpiece. Verses 31-35 are a response to the preceding verses. They are a prayer of worship.

May the glory of the LORD endure forever;
    may the LORD rejoice in his works—
who looks on the earth and it trembles,
    who touches the mountains and they smoke.
I will sing to the LORD as long as I live;
    I will sing praise to my God while I have being.
May my meditation be pleasing to him,
    for I rejoice in the LORD.
Let sinners be consumed from the earth,
    and let the wicked be no more.
Bless the LORD, O my soul.
Praise the LORD!

God's people throughout the ages have been inspired to worship God by reading this psalm. Today, how will you respond to seeing the greatness of our Creator God pictured in this psalm? Such worship is vital in our day and age. We live in an era where the glorious tapestry of God's creation is unraveling around us. As tragic as this is, we still have every reason to rejoice in our God's handiwork. The wonder of a child can and must remain with us. It can be a crucial aspect of our worship of the Lord.

Perhaps one way to nurture this sense of worship would be to write your own psalm. A psalm that celebrates creation, like Psalm 104, does two things. First, it tells what the psalm writer likes about creation. Second, it demonstrates a recognition that it is God who is the Creator of such splendid things. Take a minute right now to circle something you've already recorded that you might like to write a psalm about later. When you write your psalm in praise of the Creator God, remember to include both parts—what you like about creation and your adoration of the Maker. This can be a great Sunday afternoon activity for children and parents to do together. Plan a time when your family can gather around the kitchen table to write a common psalm about creation and the Creator.

Not only does God want us to praise him for his creation, but he also wants us to help take care of it. Psalm 104 may be thought of as a poetical commentary on the first chapter of Genesis, which describes God's creation of the world. Genesis 1:28-29 tells how God gave the responsibility of taking care of the earth to us human beings. After reading such a moving song of worship, Psalm 104 motivates us to respect what God has made and to determine what stand we will take on behalf of his creation. Can we who honor the Creator sit still while his creation is degraded and while the works of his hands are dishonored?

There are lots of ways for both adults and children to care for creation right where we live. For example, you might clean up litter along a road, help clean up a stream or pond, sort your family's garbage for recycling, or make a compost pile. Think about one thing you might like to do this week to take care of God's creation. This is another activity that adults and children can do together. As our children watch us and join with us in caring for creation, they will learn that there are adults for whom creation's care is a matter of discipleship and worship.

In closing, let's pray:

O LORD, how manifold are your works!
   In wisdom you have made them all;
   the earth is full of your creatures.

We will sing to you, O LORD, as long as we live;
    we will sing praise to you, O God, while we have being.
Thank you, O LORD, that the greatness of your creation
causes us to praise you with childlike wonder!
    Amen.

Prayer, Praise, and Play

Eugene H. Peterson

When Israel went forth from Egypt,
   the house of Jacob from a people of strange language,
Judah became his sanctuary,
   Israel his dominion.
The sea looked and fled,
   Jordan turned back.
The mountains skipped like rams,
   the hills like lambs.
What ails you, O sea, that you flee?
   O Jordan, that you turn back?
O mountains, that you skip like rams?
   O hill, like lambs?
Tremble, O earth, at the presence of the LORD,
   at the presence of the God of Jacob,
who turns the rock into a pool of water,
   the flint into a spring of water.
                    —Psalm 114 (RSV)

The most striking thing about Psalm 114 is its imagery: the sea fleeing and Jordan running away, the mountains and hills skipping like rams and lambs, the rock and flint gushing streams of water. This is prayer that is immersed in an awareness of the creation, at home in the earth, sensitive to the life of the nonhuman aspects of the environment.

On second look, it turns out that the prayer is not about nature but about history: an event—the Exodus from Egypt—is being prayed. On further examination, we find that there are, in fact, no "nature" psalms—psalms about or addressed to nature—in Scripture.

There are psalms in which our experience with and knowledge of sky and sea, animals and birds are used in the vocabulary of prayer, but it is always something about God, not creation, that is being prayed. Psalmists praise his act of creation (33); express awe at his incredible condescension in including humans in a responsible position (8); juxtapose the twin glories of sky and law to reveal God's design (19); marvel at the scheme of providence so impressively worked out in the intricate interrelations of light, wind, cloud, oceans, springs, birds, fish, storks, badgers, people at work, and people at praise (104). But the psalms are never about nature; always they are about God.

The biblical poets did not go in for "nature appreciation." In fact, they were vehemently opposed to it. Their opposition was quite deliberate, for the Hebrews' neighbors all prayed to nature. The most prominent aspects of nature are fecundity and destruction: the hidden processes of birth in earth and womb on the one hand, and on the other hand, the terrible forces of volcano, earthquake, and storm that are quite beyond any prediction or control. The Canaanites (all the surrounding nations in the extrabiblical world were much the same) were in awe of and prayed to this divinity that was beyond them. It is easy to see why they did it, for in unguarded moments we do it still. It is not easy to account for why the Hebrews chose another style of worship.

The created world around us is wondrous. Any moment that we attend to it, feelings and thoughts are roused that take us out of ourselves, feelings and thoughts that seem very much like prayer. These are so spontaneous and uncontrived, so authentic and unpretentious, that there is little doubt that we are in some deep communion with a reality beyond us, with gods— or God. Compared to our experience in the scheduled hours of worship at established places of prayer, these sometimes seem *more* genuine, which accounts perhaps for the frequently voiced preference for sunsets on the beach over eighteenth-century hymns in chapel.

But when we return to such natural settings in order to recover such feelings, what ordinarily happens is that we become more attentive to our feelings than to God. We have crossed a line. We are not praying but "using" nature to produce religious feelings. By engaging in the proper rituals and with a little bit of luck, we can manipulate nature for selfish benefit.

This is the origin of the antiprayer called magic. Prayer is willingness practiced before God; magic is willfulness exercised on nature. Magic is the skilled use of natural means to manipulate the supernatural (whether God or devil) in order to bend the natural to respond to my will. The magician is expert in using the lore of herbs, the movements of planets, the incantation of sounds, the concoction of potions, the making of diagrams (all from the realm of nature) in order to impose his or her will on nature. In the days of the psalmists, this religion was Baalism. Today this religion surfaces in one form of technology or another (*using* nature to orchestrate a lust for feelings, *using* nature to satisfy a lust for power, and so forth).

The account in 1 Kings 18, in which the priests of Baal gashed themselves with stones so that their blood flowed, is an attempt to influence the skies by magic. If they could only make the vital, life-carrying liquid from their bodies flow in sufficient quantity, surely the energy-carrying fire from the sky-god Baal would also flow. Elijah, by contrast, does not *do* anything. In prayer we do not act; *God does*. In prayer we do not develop a technology that sets the gears and pulleys of miracle in motion; we participate in God's action: "Not my will but yours."

Modern technologists are successors to pagan magicians. The means have changed, but the spirit is the same: metal machines and psychological methods have replaced magic potions, but the intent is still to work my will on the creation, regardless. God is *not* in on it, or he *is* in on it only insofar as he can be used in ways that accommodate the lordly self.

The Scene of God's Action

Psalm 114, meanwhile, holds the focus on prayer, not magic. It deals with the way God is acting with creation as his accomplice. There is nothing here about how we can manipulate nature in order to shape history to our convenience. The earth is not here for us to use; the earth is the scene of God's action. In pride we approach nature to use it; in prayer the psalmist directs us to join it in praise and celebration of God's salvation.

When Israel went forth from Egypt,
  the house of Jacob from a people of strange language,
Judah became his sanctuary,
  Israel his dominion.
              —vv. 1-2

The most unobtrusive words in these lines, the pronouns, are the very ones that turn out to be most important: *his* sanctuary, *his* dominion; that is, *God's* sanctuary, *God's* dominion. The formative experience for Israel's identity, the Exodus, is not arrogantly held up as a nationalist banner behind which the people can march, boasting of their superiority. What is expressed instead is unpretentious submission to God's gracious rule. Geography (Judah) becomes liturgy (sanctuary). A piece of land in the ancient East becomes an arena in which the divine action is played out. The two ways that we commonly use to locate ourselves in reality (where we are and what we see) are subsumed into things both larger and more intimate: God's presence and God's action. History and geography are gathered into worship.

The biblical, praying mind does not reduce place to a matter of geography—mapping and analyzing—nor to a matter of economics—assigning ownership. Rather, it views place in terms of God's presence and action in our environment. The biblical, praying mind does not abstract God from nature. Rocks and rivers, whales and elephants are participating elements in salvation. God is not understood by means of nature but nature by means of God. Creation is not pronounced divine and so made to bear more freight than she can hold, so that at one moment, gripped by fearful superstitions, we cower before her;

at another, infatuated with mental illusions, we coyly court her. Nor is God reduced to nature so that we can "handle" him, convinced that if we only learn the right technique we can use him for our purposes.

Something more like a sacrament is realized: the Exodus from Egypt and the entrance into Canaan are the means that God used to make himself known and become present to his people. He did not do this apart from history taking place in specific geography. The land and its scenery are not means that the people use to influence God but the material structure of his action among them. They pray to *him,* not to a divine stone. They pray to *him*, not a petrified god.

The difference between a sacrament and an idol (or an amulet, incantation, ritual, or figurine) is that a sacrament is what God uses to give and an idol is what we use to get. The material is involved in either case, but before the sacrament we are willing, and before the idol we are willful. Sacraments are, therefore, everyday material (rivers and lambs; water, bread, wine) because God uses whatever is commonly at hand to share himself with us. Idols, in contrast, are exceptional material—precious metals fashioned into impressive shapes, unusual objects like meteorites that will supplement our willfulness and add potency to our aspirations after lordship. When, though, we attend sacramentally to God, he uses our awareness to throw a widening light across the environment that shows Egypt and Palestine (and America) as material places where God acts redemptively.

A Way of Victory

The way in which this sacramental sense shapes our relation to our environment is expressed in the middle lines of the prayer.

The sea looked and fled,
    Jordan turned back.
The mountains skipped like rams,
    the hill like lambs.
        —vv. 3-4

At one level, this is simply a colorful account of the Exodus: "The sea looked and fled." In the more sober language of prose, this is the story of Israel. Fleeing from the Egyptians and then blocked at the waters of the Red Sea, the people walked through on dry land after Moses struck the waters with his staff and the waters parted. God "provided a way of escape." "Jordan turned back" remembers Israel's being prevented by the formidable Jordan River from entering the Promised Land at the conclusion of her forty years' wilderness trek. Then Joshua struck the waters with his staff, the river parted, and the people marched through and began their conquest of the land. God provided a way of victory. In the poetry of the psalmist "the mountains skipped like rams, the hills like lambs" is the story of the long wait of the people at the base of Sinai—the people standing in awe before the volcano-rumbling and earthquake-shaking mountain, while Moses was on the heights receiving the law.

Why not say it plainly? For one thing, God's action and presence among us is so beyond our comprehension that sober description and accurate definition are no longer functional. The levels of reality here are so beyond us that they invite extravagance of language. But the language, though extravagant, is not exaggerated. All language is inadequate and falls short. The picture of the Red Sea as a fleeing jackal, the Jordan as a cowardly sentinel forsaking his post, the Sinai as frolicking rams and lambs, is not, of course, a journalistic account of what happened, but neither is it the fabrication of an unhinged imagination. The somersaulting of what everyone had assumed to be the limitations of reality (the Red Sea and the Jordan River) and the unexpected outpouring of energy where there was nothing but a huge, dead, granite outcropping in the dead desert (Sinai) called for the new use of old words.

Wendell Berry says it well: "The earth is not dead, like the concept of property, but is as vividly and intricately alive as a man or a woman and . . . there is a delicate interdependence between its life and our own." And so the imaginative statement "the mountains skip like rams" is not mere illustration to portray the exuberance of the Sinai revelation. It is a penetrating realization that the earth itself responds to and participates in the revelation. Paul used a different, though just as striking, image for the action—"We know that the whole creation has been groaning as in the pains of childbirth right up to the present time. Not only so, but we ourselves" (Romans 8:22-23). Metaphor and simile do not explain; they draw us from being outsiders into being insiders, involved with all reality spoken into being by God's word.

Tremble, O Earth

The personal that is at the heart of the natural is expressed in the final stanza.

Tremble, O earth, at the presence of the LORD,
    at the presence of the God of Jacob,
who turns the rock into a pool of water,
    the flint into a spring of water.
                    —vv. 7-8

Tremble here reaches for the transcendental: awed respect, reverent humility. Promethean man trembles before neither earth nor altar; he takes charge. Technological man trembles before neither forest nor angel host; he operates his calculator unemotionally with steady hands. People at prayer tremble, along with the whole creation that "waits in eager expectation" (Romans 8:19) and in hopeful adoration before the mystery of creation and redemption in which "in all things God works for the good" (Romans 8:28).

Paul attempted to trace the process with the ponderous theological terms *predestination, justification, glorification*. Later he returned to the more fundamental language of prayer. "Oh, the depth of the riches of the wisdom and knowledge of God! How unsearchable his judgments, and his paths beyond tracing out!" (Romans 11:33). Here we find ourselves closer to the reality and in the presence of God's action, rather than just thinking about it.

Trembling is not, as outsiders so often think, being scared in the presence of God. It is something more like a holy playfulness, like faith frolicking. "Nature" is commonly viewed as a vast mathematical structure of cause and effect, the skies and oceans governed by rod-of-iron rules. Anyone who dares defy them is broken in pieces like a potter's vessel. According to the iron rod of gravity, for instance, my leg shatters when I fall out of a tree. According to the iron rule of thermodynamics, my finger burns as I retrieve my fork from the fire.

Prayer is not defiant or dismissive of these necessities but instead knows that there is more than necessity in the creation; there is also freedom. Prayer understands that we do not live in an ironclad universe of cause and effect. In the presence of the God of Jacob, there is life that is beyond prediction. There is freedom to change, to become more than we were in the presence of the God who "turns the rock into a pool of water, the flint into a spring of water."

Miracles are not interruptions of laws that must then either be denied by worried intellectuals or defended by anxious apologists. They are expressions of freedom enjoyed by the children of a wise and exuberant Father. We do not solve these things with rigorous exegesis of the biblical text or with controlled experiments in a laboratory; we *pray* them, and in praying enter into dimensions of personal freedom in the universe. At some level (probably beyond the level of academic comprehension, although not necessarily—the writings of the "new physics" are unexpectedly illuminative of these truths), we are in a dance. In it, necessity and freedom are synchronized and responsive to each other, each dependent on the other, alive and personal.

Our True Home

We do not begin life on our own. We do not finish it on our own. Life, especially when we experience by faith the complex interplay of creation and salvation, is not fashioned out of our own genetic lumber and cultural warehouses. It is not hammered together with the planks and nails of our thoughts and dreams, our feelings and fancies. We are not self-sufficient. We enter a world that is created by God, that already has a rich history and is crowded with committed participants—a world of animals and mountains, of politics and religion; a world where people build houses and raise children, where volcanos erupt lava, and rivers flow to the sea; a world in which, no matter how carefully we observe and watch and study it, surprising things keep on taking place (like rocks turning into pools of water). We keep on being surprised because we are in on something beyond our management, something over our heads.

In prayer we realize and practice our part in this intricate involvement with absolutely everything that is, no matter how remote it seems to us or how indifferent we are to it. This prayer is not an emotional or aesthetic sideline that we indulge in after our real work is done; it is the connective tissue of our far-flung existence. The world of creation interpenetrates the world of redemption. The world of redemption interpenetrates the world of creation. The extravagantly orchestrated skies and the exuberantly fashioned earth are not background to provide a little beauty on the periphery of the godlike ego. They are the large beauty in which we find our true home, room in which to live the cross and Christ expansively, openhearted in praise.

Of Whales and Polar Bears

Philip Yancey

Earth is crammed with heaven
And every bush aflame with God
But only those who see take off their shoes.
—Elizabeth Barrett Browning

I admit that I'm a soft touch for the Argument from Design. For me, the world of nature bears spectacular witness to the imaginative genius of our Creator. Consider these examples that I encountered on a trip to Alaska:

• A nearly invisible ice fish swims among the icebergs of Arctic and Antarctic waters, its survival made possible by the unique properties of its blood. A special protein acts as an antifreeze to keep ice crystals from forming, and its blood has no hemoglobin, or red pigments. As a result, the fish is virtually transparent.

• The instinctive navigational ability of common ducks, geese, and swans makes them the envy of the aircraft industry. On their trips south, some of the geese maintain a speed of fifty miles per hour and fly one thousand miles before making their first rest stop.

• When it comes to navigation, polar bears are no slouches either. A polar bear that is tranquilized, trapped, and released three hundred miles away from home can usually find its way back, even across drift ice that changes constantly and holds no landmarks and few odors. But bears and birds are rank amateurs compared to lowly salmon, who cruise the expanse of the Pacific Ocean for several years before returning (by scent? magnetic field?) to the streams of their birth.

• Baby musk oxen are born in March and April, when temperatures still languish around 30 below zero. Thus, as the tiny musk ox drops two feet to the ground, its surrounding temperature drops 130 degrees. The mother must hasten to lick blood and fluid from the coat of the steaming calf lest it freeze. Within a few minutes, the calf staggers to its feet and begins to nurse.

• Comparatively, grizzlies and polar bears have it easy. Ursine mothers feel no pain when giving birth for the simple reason that birthing takes place in the dead of winter, hibernation time. The cub struggles through the birth canal, pokes around the new world, and figures out the nursing process on its own. (Imagine the mother bear's surprise when spring rolls around.)

• One more fact about polar bears. For years it puzzled researchers that polar bears and harp seals never showed up on the aerial infrared photographs used in animal censuses. Yet both species showed up very clearly on ultraviolet photographs, even though white objects normally reflect, rather than absorb, ultraviolet light rays. In 1978, a United States Army researcher discovered the reason. Polar bear hairs are not white at all, but transparent. Under a scanning electron microscope they appear as hollow tubes, without pigment. They act like tiny fiberoptic tubes, trapping the warming ultraviolet rays and funneling them to the bear's body. At the same time, the fur provides such efficient insulation that the bear's outer temperature stays virtually the same as the surrounding ice. This explains why bears do not show up on infrared photos.

When I learn such details about the natural world, I feel like writing a hymn in honor of the polar bear or musk ox. Such a hymn has good precedent: In his majestic speech at the end of the book of Job, God himself pointed to the wonders of creation as compelling proof of his power and wisdom. When he and Job compared resumes, Job ended up repenting in dust and ashes.

As I say, I'm a soft touch for the Argument from Design. Still, I must acknowledge that not everyone responds to nature in the same way. As novelist Walker Percy has observed, "There may be signs of [God's] existence, but they point both ways and are therefore ambiguous and so prove nothing. . . . The wonders of the universe do not convince those most conversant with the wonders, the scientists themselves."

Why isn't the Argument from Design more convincing? Percy is right: Nature gives off mixed signals. I left Alaska with sentiments of worship and admiration; the polar bears' prey probably had a different perspective. And I might have been less anxious to write a hymn had I pondered instead the design of Alaskan mosquitoes or the Cecidomyian gall midge (whose young hatch inside their mother and literally eat their way out, devouring the mother as they go).

Like humanity, the rest of the created world presents a strange mixture of beauty and horror, of splendid cooperation and savage competition. In the apostle Paul's words, "We know that the whole creation has been groaning as in the pains of childbirth right up to the present time" (Romans 8:22). Nature is our fallen sister, not our mother.

C. S. Lewis said that the Christian does not go to nature to learn theology—the message is too garbled—but rather to fill theological words with meaning: "Nature never taught me that there exists a God of glory and of infinite majesty. I had to learn that in other ways. But nature gave the word *glory* a meaning for me. I still do not know where else I could have found one."

I didn't learn much theology on my trip to Alaska. But wading in a glacial stream dyed red with spawning salmon and watching a bald eagle pluck a sea bass out of the bay, I did fill a few words with meaning. Words like *joy* and *awe*.

Just a few miles outside Anchorage, as I drove along the oddly named inlet, Turnagain Arm, I noticed a number of cars pulled off the highway. When Alaskan cars pull over, that usually means animals. Against the slate-gray sky, the water of Turnagain Arm appeared to have a slight greenish cast, interrupted by small whitecaps. Soon I saw these were not whitecaps at all, but whales—silvery white beluga whales. A pod was feeding no more than fifty feet offshore.

I stood for forty minutes, listening to the rhythmic motion of the sea, following the graceful, ghostly crescents of surfacing whales. The crowd was hushed, even reverent. We passed around binoculars, saying nothing, simply watching. More cars pulled off the road. Dogs chased each other on the shoreline, their owners oblivious. For just that moment, nothing else—dinner reservations, the trip schedule, my life back in Chicago—mattered.

We were confronted with a scene of quiet beauty and a majesty of scale. We all felt small. We stood together in silence until the whales moved farther out. And then we climbed the bank together and got in our cars to resume our busy, ordered lives, which somehow seemed less urgent.

And it wasn't even Sunday.

Part Six

How Can I Challenge My Congregation to Get Involved?

In 1988, the drama of the Fifteenth Winter Olympics gripped all America. Speed skater Dan Jansen was our hero. Millions of hopes for a gold medal or two chased him around the rink with each lap. These hopes faded as Dan fell on the ice and, a few days later, fell again.

The reasons for Dan's tumbles were well known. His sister, Jane, had died of a terminal illness before his first race. He had a lot on his mind: his loving and supportive family as well as his previous spills, which seemed to snowball into additional falls on the ice. Still, Dan got up and kept skating. He could say after each race that his family would know that he had skated his best.

The church of Jesus Christ is certainly running a race. We strive to live out the gospel in our world. "Let us run with perseverance the race marked out for us" (Hebrews 12:1). Can we pause for a moment to ask ourselves how the race is going in this arena of caring for creation? I do not believe that the church is living up to its calling at all. The Bible's mandate to care for creation is clear, but unfortunately the church's lack of involvement is equally obvious. Sure, we have a lot on our minds, just as Dan Jansen did. We live in a very complex age. So many needs call out to us. Nonetheless, our Creator has made his will quite clear. Disciples are to care for the earth.

Can we get back up off the ice? Can we recover from our tumbles? And what can we *do*? These concluding sermons of *The Best Preaching on Earth* provide challenge and insight into moving beyond thinking about and talking about creation care, to a place of action.

"Do not merely listen to the word, and so deceive yourselves. Do what it says" (James 1:22, emphasis added).

The Good Earth. Dr. Brand's delightful sermon relates creation care to our daily walk with Christ as disciples. He concludes by asking some convicting questions. What sort of spiritual heritage are we passing on to our children and grandchildren? What kind of physical heritage are we leaving our children?

The Price of Gopher Wood. This short piece is one of the editor's favorites. It is a straightforward message that challenges our level of commitment to God's will. Calvin DeWitt holds up the story of Noah as an example to us. This Old Testament servant of God paid a great price for his faithfulness to God's call to care for creation. In this age of creation's degradation, our commitments may place as many demands on us as Noah's did on him. May *we* show the same faithfulness to biblical earth keeping to our world and to our Maker!

Because He Came: The Surprising Implications of Christmas. Biblical faith is utterly focused on Jesus Christ. From this core of our faith—from the life of Jesus Christ—we find compelling reasons to be actively involved in caring for creation. The Creator God, taking on created flesh, calls us to serious engagement in the world and on behalf of creation.

I Shop, Therefore I Am. It is so easy to point a finger at the overpopulated nations of the world and to believe that these countries are bringing our planet to ruin. It is harder to understand the role that *we* play in degrading creation. Jim Wallis helps us see that caring for creation involves understanding how our lifestyles help deplete the earth of its richness and fruitfulness. By considering the lilies of the field and the birds of the air, by understanding what is happening in our cities and in all creation, we will understand that faithful discipleship must include adjusting the way we consume. In this way, we will honor the one who has blessed us with the goodness of creation.

The Good Earth

Paul Brand

And the LORD God formed man from the dust of the
ground and breathed into his nostrils the breath of life,
and man became a living being . . . Dust you are and to
dust you will return.
—Genesis 2:7; 3:19

The simple, illiterate mountain people in India do not have
many naturalists or environmentalists to teach them how to
defend their soil. They do not need them. It is a life-and-death
matter, and they learn in childhood what they practice as adult
farmers, and then teach their grandchildren when they get too
old to farm. I have a vivid childhood memory of that process.

I was playing with a group of Indian boys in one of the rice
paddies near our home in the mountains. Rice needs flooded
fields for certain stages of its cultivation. In the absence of level
ground in the mountains, the hill tribes have developed a method
of terracing their fields into the course of a stream so that each
field is about a foot lower than the field above. These fields are
quite level, being bordered at the lower edge by a grass-covered
dam to hold water. Little channels are cut at intervals along the
dams to allow a trickle of the stream into the field below.

Thus, where the valley is steep, the fields are narrow. They
are wide where the slope is shallow. The water from the one
stream flows into each field in turn and keeps the mud wet
enough for rice cultivation. The constant wetness is attractive to
frogs and small fish and also to herons, who came after the frogs.
Not only herons but small boys enjoy the mud and the frogs, so
it happened that my friends and I were having a game to see who

would be the first to catch three frogs. This involved a lot of plunging about in the mud in the corner of one of the fields.

Suddenly the oldest boy called out, "Tata is coming!" and we all scrambled out of the mud. *Tata* means grandfather and is used by youngsters as a term of respect for any elderly man. The particular tata we had seen coming our way was the owner of one of the fields and was recognized as the keeper of the dams. He was the one who saw to it that nobody got more than his fair share of water when the stream was running low. We all knew that we had not been careful with the rice seedlings, and we deserved and expected a rebuke.

Tata was very old and stooped over. He found it difficult to look straight forward. He walked slowly with a cane, but none of us thought of running away or of avoiding his stern words. Old age carries much respect in India. He asked us what we were doing, and the biggest boy, acting as our spokesman, told him we had been catching frogs. Tata looked at the churned up mud, then stooped over and scooped up a double handful of it.

"What is this?" he asked.

"That is mud, Tata," we replied.

"And whose mud is it?"

"It is your mud, Tata, and we have broken your seedlings. We are very sorry, and we will never do it again."

But Tata had more to say. "There is enough mud in my hands to grow a whole meal of rice for one person. This same mud will grow a meal of rice every year. It has been doing it for my parents and grandparents long before I was born. It will go on growing rice for my grandchildren and their children for many generations."

"Yes, Tata."

Then the old man moved over to the nearest of the water channels across the earthen dam. He pointed to it. "What do you see there?" he asked.

"That is water," replied our spokesman.

For the first time the old man showed his anger. "I'll show you water," he growled, and limped on a few steps to the next channel, where clear water was flowing over the grass. "*That* is water," he said, and returned to the first channel. "Now tell me what you see here."

"That is mud, Tata," the boy said humbly. "It is muddy water." Then he hurried on to tell Tata what he knew would come next, for he had been exposed to this before. "This is your mud that is running down to the lower field, and it will never grow food for you again because mud never runs uphill. Once it has gone, it is gone forever."

Tata wanted to make sure we all got the message. Leaning on his staff, he straightened his back as far as he could, so he could look at each one of us. "When you see mud running in the streams of water, you know that life is running out of the mountains. It will never come back." He turned and began to limp away, softly repeating to himself, "It will never come back."

That was seventy-five years ago, but I have never forgotten the lesson I learned that day. It is a universal truth. Even in America, mud never runs uphill. When we see erosion taking away our topsoil, life is flowing away from our homeland.

It will never come back . . . It will never come back.

I have also learned to respect the way folk wisdom is passed from generation to generation in lands that have no schools. One of the boys I was playing with that day is probably called Tata" today, and he is patrolling the paddy fields, striking fear into the hearts of small boys and making sure that the mud of life stays in the mountains to bear fruit.

What I saw on a small scale in a mountain paddy field in India we see on a massive and tragic scale in Nepal and on the slopes of the Himalayas. For thousands of years, a sturdy, simple people have lived high on those mountain slopes. Most of them live in well-watered valleys between mountain ranges. Over the centuries, the Nepalese have farmed the valleys and have grown crops on the little ledges, where trees have held the soil wherever the slope was shallow enough for their roots to cling.

Today the population has increased, and farming has become more commercialized and aggressive. There are more cattle and goats for milk, and they have to go further to graze. More trees are cut for firewood and for homes. The wooded slopes are becoming bare. The soil is suddenly free to move, and it is moving. The rivers that once were clear are now full of mud.

Bangladesh, a country of fertile plains, has always been subject to flooding when the snows are melting on the Himalayas. The monsoon rains and melted snow fill the great rivers of the Ganges and Brahmaputra. In the past few years, and especially last year, the problem reached a new scale. Not only did the rivers overflow, but the flood was not just water— it was *mud*. Homes in Bangladesh were filled with mud. People drowned in mud. That mud was Nepali soil. It had grown crops for generations of mountain people, and now it was gone forever. It will never come back, and more is being lost every year. There are more people every year who depend on the crops that have less soil to grow in. Soil is eroding all over the world, and most of the problem is created by human actions and is preventable. It is one of the great tragedies of all time, and little is being done to halt the loss. This crisis is part of a pattern of the worship of money and mindless disregard for God's earth. We who claim to serve the Creator should be asking ourselves whether we are being good stewards of his great gifts.

"A Farmer Went Out to Sow His Seed"

I feel a bit like Tata. I do not have a farm, but I try to pass on to others the lessons I have learned about soil and water and about our duty to God, who left us as stewards of his earth. When God planted the garden of Eden and handed to Adam the title deed, his only instructions were, "Work it and take care of it" (Genesis 2:15). We have edited that document so that it seems to read, "Exploit it for profit."

I see myself as a farmer of spiritual soil, a sower of spiritual seed. Jesus spoke about making his disciples to become fishers of men, but more often he used the picture of sowers of seed and talked about good soil and farmers.

Even as God the Creator brought life and the soil together to make the first man, so in the continuity of spiritual life, the seed and the soil have to come together to create new life and then to continue life and growth by drawing nourishment from the soil as long as life continues. To illustrate these truths, Jesus told the parable of the sower and the seed. It could be titled the parable of the seed and the *soil,* because the only variable in the parable was the soil. The seed and the sower were the same throughout the parable. The fruitfulness or lack of it resulted from where and into what kind of soil the seed was sown.

> A farmer went out to sow his seed. As he was scattering the seed, some fell along the path; it was trampled on, and the birds of the air ate it up.
> —Luke 8:5

A pathway is never a good place to plant seed. Human feet beat down the soil, smoothing out any crevices into which the seed can fall and germinate. The soil becomes hardened, and any seed that falls there will not find that openness necessary for life and growth.

In such situations, the devil is quick to snatch the seed away. In a spiritual sense, such people have their hearts hardened. The author of Hebrews pleads with his readers, "Today, if you hear his voice, do not harden your hearts *(harden your soil?)* as you did in the rebellion . . . " (Hebrews 3:7-8). He was referring to the time when the Israelites were offered a chance to enter the promised land but turned back because they did not believe God could or would see them through. The prospect of difficulties and battles ahead made them close their minds and harden their hearts to all God had in store for them.

Living seed and sprouting wheat are not willing to share their piece of earth with booted feet. If the earth is to be a path, it might as well be paved. If it is to be soil, it must allow the seed to take over and draw nourishment and support from it. To accept the seed, soil has to become involved.

In a physical sense, there is a choice that has to be made in the use of the land. It may be used as a farm to grow food, or it may become a road and be paved for buildings and travel. The priorities of a community are revealed by the choices it makes.

Today in America, prime farmland is being paved at a record rate to make way for roads and cities. Two and a half million hectares of cropland were lost to paving and building in the United States in an eight-year period in the seventies.

Perhaps a similar change is taking place in our mental and spiritual outlooks. Mechanical and commercial development thrives on hard surfaces. Spiritual and personal priorities need a softer soil, one that is vulnerable and open to suggestions and ideas that may require personal involvement. Jesus looks to us, his messengers, to prepare soil by taking time to plow and hoe and soften it before we plant the seed.

Used or Used Up?

> Some fell on rocky places, where it did not have much soil. It sprang up quickly, because the soil was shallow. But when the sun came up, the plants were scorched, and they withered because they had no root.
> —Matthew 13:5-6

A farm is often defined by its size or extent. "For Sale: 500-acre farm in southern Iowa. Has been used for corn and soybeans." I would not buy that farm until I knew a lot more about it. The words *has been used* may have many implications. Good soil, farmed by good farmers, can grow food for many generations, as Tata knew well. Iowa had deep, rich topsoil when serious farming started in the last century. Today more than 50 percent of that topsoil has been lost. Much of it has been carried down the river into the Gulf of Mexico.

As topsoil becomes thinner, crops become more and more dependent on frequent rainfall and on fertilizers. Good farmers plow back most of the stalks and leaves from each harvest and thus enrich the soil, actually building it up year by year. If "shallow soil" refers to the person who has little background knowledge of Scripture or scant experience of Christian fellowship, then we should be careful to follow the planting of the seed with fellowship and instruction in Scripture. The tender plant may be shielded from the scorching heat of the noon sun by the protective shade of an overarching older sister or brother in Christ.

Roots in Competition

> Other seed fell among thorns, which grew up and choked the plants. . . . The one who received the seed that fell among the thorns is the man who hears the word, but the worries of this life and the deceitfulness of wealth choke it, making it unfruitful.
> —Matthew 13:7,22

This parable doesn't suggest that the thorny soil was bad soil. It may have been excellent. But it was already occupied. It had been colonized by wild thorn bushes. Their roots had penetrated deep into the soil and were consuming the nourishment the wheat needed. Now they challenged the farmer: "Pull us out at your peril! You will have to grasp us by our thorns. It will be painful!"

In another parable Jesus said, "You cannot serve God and mammon" (Matthew 6:24 RSV). The farmer might say to this piece of soil, "Choose you this day what you will grow: thorns or wheat." Jesus is specific about the nature of the thorns; they take over and choke the good seed. Matthew says that wealth is a thorn. Luke, in his account, adds "worries, riches and pleasures" (Luke 8:14). Note that Jesus doesn't say that the good seed couldn't survive with that kind of thornbush. What he says is that the growth was unfruitful.

Rich and Fertile Soil

> But the one who received the seed that fell on good soil is the man who hears the word and understands it. He produces a crop, yielding a hundred, sixty or thirty times what was sown.
> —Matthew 13:23

When Jesus mentions the three kinds of soil that were not productive, he tells us why. He doesn't define the nature of the good soil except to say that it produced bountiful crops. Jesus hinted that some soil was better than others when he told the people that some seed produced a hundredfold, some sixty, and some thirty. The difference must have been in the soil.

Since the Bible does not give any clues about grading good soil, I feel free to broaden the parable to include one aspect of good soil that has meaning both in farming and in spiritual life. In botany, the term "colonize" refers to the way a group of plants or grasses takes over a piece of land. A good example is seen in sand dunes that have been built up by the action of tides and winds. They shift and change shape from year to year. Then seeds of some hardy type of grass may be blown into the area and begin to take root. If rain falls at the right time and roots have a chance to grow, the grasses may form a colony and begin to hold the sand together by their interlocking root systems. After a few years, the plants change the very nature of the sand and turn it into the beginnings of real soil. At a later stage, other less hardy plants may come and take root. What was once poor soil has been transformed into good and fertile soil. Eventually the original pioneer grasses may be forgotten as the plants and trees thrive.

What has been added to the original sand to turn it into soil? The simplified answer is that it is *the life and then the death of the pioneer plants.* When you study a handful of good, rich soil, you will note the numerous tiny live creatures there. They are busy breaking down fragments of leaves and decaying wood, turning them into still smaller fragments that can be a source of nitrogen and phosphorus and other good things for new living plants.

My home is near the Olympic National Park and the rain forest that clothes the lower slopes of the western mountains. We love to take our grandchildren to see the wonder of the living forest. Near the Hoh River, there is a row of trees that look as if they were planted by a landscape gardener—the trees are in a straight line. Each of those giant trees seems to be standing astride, with its legs apart. Each trunk is single but only down to about six feet above ground. At that point, the trunk is supported by two huge root systems, like legs, that spread apart and curve down to reach the ground six feet apart, leaving a tunnel between them. If you look through the tunnel of the first tree, you can see through the other tunnels in the other trees because they are in a straight line.

There is an explanation for this curious sight. A hundred years ago or more, a giant tree fell in the forest. It died and lay dead and decaying for many years. Seeds, falling from other great trees, fell into the cracks of the bark and rooted there, using the dead tree as rich soil. All the materials the old tree had collected over the years, which had formed the basis of its strength and vitality, were now being made available to the young seedlings growing on what we now call a "nursery log." As the young trees grew, they needed support for their great size, while the dead tree was weakened by decay. So the young trees sent out roots around the old trunk to reach the ground on either side. Those roots gradually became the whole support of the young trees, while the old tree disintegrated and finally disappeared, becoming one with the soil around it.

Our children and grandchildren have stood quietly looking through the space where that old tree lay. We cannot see the tree itself, but we can see the way it has helped to shape and to give nourishment to the new generation of great trees, forming a colonnade in memory of the nursery log whose substance continues in them. I look through that space, too, but with a different perspective. My active life is mostly behind me. Soon I will no longer occupy this earthly home. But I pray that my life and the principles God has helped me to live by will continue to influence young lives. When we die, we do not only leave seed; we also leave an effect on the soil in which future children will grow and future spiritual seed will be nourished. That's one reason the psalmist says, "Precious in the sight of the LORD is the death of his saints" (Psalm 116:15).

I remember sitting with my mother on the steps of the guest house at a leprosy hospital in India. We were facing east, and the sun was rising over the mountains opposite us, flooding us with early light. I was soon to leave India, and Mother had a prophetic sense that she would not see me again. At ninety-five, Mother knew she would not live much longer and was giving me instructions about the way she wanted to be buried. "Don't let them make a coffin for me," she pleaded. "Too many trees are being cut down on the hills. There's no sense in using up wood to make a box for me to be buried in. Tell them to wrap me in an old sheet—not a new one—and let them scatter flowers over my body while they lower me into the ground."

"I know they will be sad because they love me. But tell them to choose joyful hymns to sing—hymns of victory. It's not me that they will be burying, but just my old body. I am going to be with my Lord. I will not regret having my body return to the earth. It has been a good body, but it has been getting weak and stiff lately, and it's time to put it away."

I couldn't reply. We just sat together, holding hands, until the sun became too hot for comfort. We went indoors and had breakfast, and I left the hospital, never to see her again. A month or two later, she died. She was buried beside her husband in the mountains, and there was no coffin.

There is something triumphant about the death of a saint. Dust to dust, yes, but also spirit leaping up to report to God about the completion of the great adventure by which one or two hundred pounds of mud have been inspired—"in-breathed"—to be active and creative in God's service. That transformed mud has been the messenger of God and the instrument of his love for many years. Hallelujah!

I have often returned to the church my father and mother built on those mountains, and I have seen the rough-hewn headstones that mark the places, side by side, where they returned to dust. I cry because I cannot help it, but I thank God that their life goes on. It goes on in me and in my sister and in our children, who inherited their physical seed. It also goes on in the lives of those who attend that church in the mountains, where they received the spiritual seed that bore fruit and is now being passed on to the lively third generation of church members.

Good soil is the legacy of pioneer grasses and plants now long gone. It has been said that "the blood of the martyrs is the seed of the church." Perhaps it would be more accurate to say that the blood is the *soil* of the church. The seed is the living Word of God. Godly people not only plant the seed; the quality of their lives affects the environment in which those seeds will grow. I pray that all of us will do our part to leave an enriched soil that will help to grow a sturdy church. I pray also, in a reversal of the parable, that we shall all be sensitive to the physical needs of future generations. We need to repent of our willing cooperation in our money-centered culture, which is depleting the natural resources that God designed for all humankind. He gave us a *good earth*. Let us serve him by helping to preserve it for our children. "A good man leaves an inheritance for his children's children" (Proverbs 13:22).

The Price of Gopher Wood

Calvin B. DeWitt

Make thee an ark of gopher wood.
        —Genesis 6:14 (KJV)

Some stories that we came to know so well as children have scarcely been given a second thought by adults. The account of Noah is such a story. The image this tale brings to mind might include a big wooden boat, a man with a long flowing beard, lions, giraffes, zebras. The giraffes have their necks out a window, and a pair of zebras is calmly walking up the gangplank. Recalling this famous story with our mind's eye, we see animal occupants to be found now on a stroll through the zoo; there are no beetles, no frogs, no land snails.

As we clarify our mental image, we realize that we are reviewing a picture we colored with crayons in our Sunday school paper, or the animal cutouts made with scissors and crayons for placement in a paper ark.

We, the recallers of this childhood story, have become captives of this or a similar childhood image. We may rightly remember the important point that the world was bad, and that God destroyed it because of the rampant evil of the day. We no doubt also remember his promise never to send another such flood, for which promise the rainbow was given as a sign. But the critical ethical and ecological relevance of the story for today's world is obscure; we are captives of a paper ark in a child's world.

Familiarity with our childhood image gives an illusion of understanding. Impressed that we already know, we fail to give this story the attention it deserves today. A major point of the story rarely has entered the adult mind.

The element missing from our understanding of the Noah account was made clear to me by the reaction of a Christian college student returning from a trip to observe the Kirtland's Warbler preservation project in northern Lower Michigan: "What a waste to spend all that time, energy, and money to try to save a tiny bird."

God made it clear to Noah that he cared so much for the creatures he had created that he wanted each one of them to be saved from impending extinction. He asked Noah to build a large boat out of gopher wood—at great cost of time, energy, and materials—to save not only himself and his family but also the other creatures. Concerns about time or money apparently were not raised by Noah. Neither were questions about the significance or worthiness of each species. Noah did as the Lord commanded him.

How much less time-consuming and less expensive it would have been to build a smaller boat! Why not just a boat for Noah and family? Or why not a boat for them and only the animals of use to them?

My response to the student returning from the Kirtland's Warbler country was: "Yes, the price of gopher wood is very high these days. Certainly we could find something more productive on which to spend our time and money!" Knowing the Noah account very well from childhood, she paused thoughtfully and replied, "I get the point, and it is a very good one!"

As in Noah's day, there is again a deluge moving across the land. Of course, God has remained true to his promise, to his covenant; all life has not again been eliminated by a great flood. But we have not been true to God and the preservation of his creatures. We are part of the human tide that is sweeping across the world, eliminating the creatures in the path of our use and abuse of the world's resources. As part of this flood, we even have found reason to criticize and ridicule those few who work to preserve God's creatures from extinction.

While a few speak out against the destruction of the creatures, many others work to convert the creatures into personal profits. Living in the gallery of the Great Artist, a small minority cry out against the destruction of his creative works; others work diligently to convert the treasury of the creatures into cold cash. The elephants are slaughtered so their great teeth can be reworked into ivory ornaments by human artists; the seals are killed so the coverings that protect them in the cold Arctic waters can adorn our women of fashion; the tropical birds are destroyed to provide the feathers for our hats; rare animals are wrenched from their native homes and sold to be placed behind bars in our cities; the great whales are hunted to extinction with ever more sophisticated ships to provide a trickle of whale oil, perfume, and meat for the marketplace.

This careless extinguishing of species in pursuit of human greed runs counter to the value the Creator puts on his creatures. God brings praise to himself through the creatures he has made. Concerning Behemoth, God asks Job and us to give him and his creatures due respect.

Behold, Behemoth,
    which I made as I made you;
    he eats grass like an ox.
Behold, his strength in his loins,
    and his power in the muscles of his belly.
He makes his tail stiff like a cedar;
    the sinews of his thighs are knit together.
His bones are like tubes of bronze,
    his limbs like bars of iron.
He is the first of the works of God;
    let him who made him bring near his sword!
            —Job 40:15-19 (RSV)

But the direct assault on individual species of the creation pales against the flood of lumbering that is raging through the tropical rain forests of the world. In pursuit of the work of our Creator and the integrated beauty of these magnificent forests, to convert them into plywood for our boats and homes, the homes of the creatures are being destroyed forever. Carefully tuned cycles of forest nutrients are broken by laying bare the tropics. Nutrients once reinjected into trunks and leaves by the vibrant forests are irretrievably lost to erosion and percolation. The homes of the creatures are destroyed, and thus also its creatures. The gallery of the Great Artist is being trashed. The great treasury of the creation is being converted to ash.

Where are the Noahs? Where are the courses and curricula in ark building? The whole creation is standing on tippy toes, waiting . . . !

Because He Came: The Surprising Implications of Christmas

Dwight Ozard

Your attitude should be the same as that of Christ Jesus:
Who, being in very nature God,
   did not consider equality with God something to be grasped,
but made himself nothing,
   taking the vary nature of a servant,
   being made in human likeness.
And being found in appearance as a man,
   he humbled himself
and became obedient to death
      —even death on a cross!
Therefore God exalted him to the highest place
   and gave him the name that is above every name,
that at the name of Jesus every knee should bow,
   in heaven and on earth and under the earth,
and every tongue confess that Jesus Christ is Lord,
   to the glory of God the Father.
      —Philippians 2:5-11

Other texts: Luke 3:1-14; John 3:16

Introduction

My Dad is a preacher, so I grew up with all the advantages and disadvantages of being a PK, including oddly scheduled times for father-son days. He was committed to spending time with me but rarely had evenings free. So I became used to my dad trying to find time for us in bits between commitments in his busy schedule, and I was rarely surprised by off-beat requests for early morning walks or a game of catch squeezed between supper and Wednesday night prayer meeting. So when on a Saturday morning the November I was seven, my father asked me to go with him to the church office that afternoon and watch him conduct a wedding, I did not think it terribly odd.

But it was also out of the question. He wasn't the only one with a busy schedule. Saturday afternoons were sacred on the streets of our Toronto suburb—street hockey ruled. And besides, I knew that the late afternoon wedding would stretch into an early evening supper, and that would mean getting home after 8:00 P.M., when "Hockey Night" in Canada started. I put my foot down. Unfortunately, so did my father, and soon my mother did, too.

"Why?" I protested. "Why should I go and sit in Dad's study and do nothing *forever* while I wait for him?"

"Because," my Dad implored, "I want you to."

"*Please*," my mother joined. They were begging. There was clearly no good reason to go. It was the first time in my life I realized that I could reason with—indeed, *out*-reason—my parents. I dug my heels in. They offered bribes—a special edition of *Moby Dick*—and gave me that to bide my time.

"Please do what your mother asks you, Son." My father's voice was pathetic. "It will be worth it, and I promise you, you won't miss the game."

I didn't believe him. But he was my dad. I spent an excruciating *eon* in my father's office, pasting stickers of Ishmael, Ahab, and the Great White Whale in my new book. When we got in the car after the wedding, my dad turned the wrong way on the highway. We weren't going home.

"I have to pick something up downtown at the Bible Society," he said. Traffic was dense, and I asked why. "I guess everyone's going to the game."

Sure, rub salt in the wound. We were going to get home late

for sure, and my sister would have the TV monopolized. No hockey.

We finally parked, and my dad took my hand and walked me through Toronto's busy downtown streets. Dad pointed up through the crowd.

"Isn't that Maple Leaf Gardens? Why don't we go see if we can get an autograph?"

I was seven and had no idea that Dave Keon, Bob Pulford, and Johnnie Bower got to the rink at 5:00 P.M., not 7:30 P.M., for an 8:00 P.M. game. The allure of meeting a player almost made up for not seeing the game.

As we approached the main entrance, my dad looked down at me, reached into his pocket, and handed me an envelope. I thought it was for autographs, but he said, "Look inside."

And there they were. The two most beautiful pieces of paper ever printed on. Tickets. Tickets to see the Toronto Maple Leafs, twelve rows from the ice, dead center, simply the best seats in the house. It was the greatest surprise I have ever had.

Ever since then, I have loved surprises. I love a surprise party. I love a punch line that takes me unexpected places. I even love watching Oprah reunite guests with long-lost loves. And as a historian, I have loved the surprise of discovering new insights and ideas. But mostly, I think I love the surprises of Scripture, startling me with the unexpected truth of God's love.

Today we begin to celebrate the ultimate in surprises—Advent. The coming of God to this world in Christ. Most religions talk about humanity aspiring to God. Some talk about God pretending to be human. But no other religion has as surprising a story as Christianity, with its notion of the Incarnation: that God *became* Man, put on our flesh, and leapt into his creation so completely that he became indistinguishable from it in order to serve and to save it. That message is completely overwhelming.

And because of that, every year around this time, I'm saddened by a kind of Christianity that is without any messy surprises—a faith that acts as if the Advent had never occurred. It is a vision of discipleship that makes Jesus, and therefore our faith, into something distinct and apart from this world and the flesh and blood of our lives.

It seems that there are a bunch of Christians who think God would have done it a lot better if he just skipped over the whole Nativity thing. I mean, a baby in a manger isn't very efficient, and the Creator of the universe in diapers certainly doesn't reflect the power and majesty of God very well now, does it?!?

Wouldn't it have been easier for God just to appear to us all—*as God*—and really leave no doubt about his existence, will, and plan? I mean, Yahweh in the sky above Jerusalem, or Rome, or Manhattan would certainly remove all doubt.

And if you listen to what's on Christian radio or read a good percentage of the Christian books being sold by evangelicals, you might be convinced that Jesus *did* come in invincible power and strength to conquer the world as a mighty warrior—perhaps a heavenly gunslinger whose main task was to stomp the devil and establish some kind of invisible, otherworldly kingdom filled with folks whose lives and parking spots hang in the balance of some celestial sword fight. For these folks, Jesus came to simply save our souls, and to rescue us *from* the world.

And to be honest, if that *is* why Jesus came, and if Christian living *is* all about escaping the earth and getting to an immaterial heaven, then the stories of Christmas really don't make any sense. They're simply incongruent, about as relevant as Santa Claus.

But Jesus did come at Christmas. God chose to announce his love for the world, to proclaim forgiveness of sins, to inaugurate the kingdom of God, and to reconcile us to him with *a baby and a bunch of poor folk*. At Christmas we discover a God who *would not* come in power, but who instead offered himself to us in weakness and humility, and who offered himself to us *in the world*.

That offering has immediate and surprising implications for how we live out our faith. I want to talk quickly about three of the most surprising implications that the Incarnation holds for our lives, implications that will make us reconsider what it means to be a disciple in this world.

First, Christmas means that our discipleship will be fundamentally earthy.

Often when we talk about spirituality or being saved or our discipleship, we evangelicals tend to talk about something very different from the day-to-day experiences of this world. "Spiritual" things usually mean either (1) a narrow set of values and moral rules imposed from outside this world as some kind of test upon humanity or (2) the invisible realms where God lives, where we go when we die, and where all the important stuff of the universe—and of our lives—happens.

In this world-view, the earth is inconsequential—simply a stage that mirrors reality. And in this world-view, our discipleship can disown the earth, our physical world, and even our bodies, making them secondary to the *real* thing.

But a discipleship that takes Christmas seriously cannot do that. Instead, it understands that God *created* for a reason and that God entered into his creation in Christ for a reason, as well. Yes, the faith that flows from the Incarnation will embrace the mystery of the invisible and call us to deeper, greater, and unseen realities. Yes, it will speak of realms that we call "spiritual" and where our Father and his hosts exist, and it will call us to live in their light.

But the Incarnation also tells us that God made us to be *earthly* beings and calls us to a spirituality that lets us be earthly beings. In fact, the life and message of Christ make it abundantly clear that whatever our discipleship is to be, it must be about the grit, pain, intensity, diversity, beauty, brokenness, the stuff of this world; it will embrace and affirm and celebrate flesh and blood, the toil of sweat and work, the stuff of creation, and other people. The Incarnation—Christ's embrace of our humanity and coming into our world—and the resurrection—God's vindication of Christ's ministry—tell us that God has not abandoned, and will never abandon, his creation. Our hope, according to Paul, is not in rescue *from* the earth but in resurrection and restoration. Jesus came to establish the kingdom of God. *On earth.*

Too often, in an effort to keep pure and avoid the fallenness of our world, we have simply abandoned the world that God would not abandon. But the Incarnation is messy. It is *never* safe or easy. It blurs the distinction between the secular and the sacred. It deconstructs the expected categories and announces that God is here, in the midst of it all, because Jesus came and embraced it all. The Incarnation says that what is spiritual is determined not by its separation from the world as much as by the presence of God in Christ in the midst of it.

"But what of holiness?" you ask. "Isn't that separation *from* the world?"

I can only answer in one way: *No!* Holiness isn't separation from the world; it's separation *to* God, the same God who came and entered our world eating, drinking, dancing, weeping, and laughing. The same God who became a carpenter and learned to shape a piece of wood he had created. The same God who is confident enough of the reach of love that he called men and women to follow him onto the streets of his day, where prostitutes and cheats were more numerous than the godly.

This "earthy discipleship" means two things. First, *we can celebrate the good things of earth*. We don't have to divide the world into categories of secular and sacred and set up code words and special tests. The earth—"stuff"—was made for us to enjoy and use and honor and celebrate. And better, God has chosen to use it, too. His Incarnation says that no matter how fallen, broken, and miserable this world is, God has not abandoned or given up on it. We must not succumb to a theology that is so otherworldly that it denies the goodness of creation or suggests that our purposes and pleasures as human creatures should deny that creation's goodness. Jesus' embrace of our lives puts an end to both gnostic escapism and ascetic pleasure-fearing. While I do not want to suggest for a minute that the Incarnation means *everything* about the earth is fine (after all, he came to save and redeem it, not simply stamp it with his approval), I want to insist that discipleship is about the redemption of our lives on earth—never about escape from the life of earth.

This frees us to create. It frees us to trust the simple things that we do—like share a meal or shape some clay or make love to our spouse—as ways that God makes himself known to us and through us.

Second, earthy discipleship means *we can serve right where he has "planted" us.* We can be confident that whatever God has called us to do, it will involve our lives and our world.

When I went back to university after having been in "full-time" ministry for a year, I was haunted by the notion that I was forsaking my calling. My first week back, I met a girl I had gone to public school with. We hadn't seen each other in twelve years, but we quickly became fast friends. She was not a Christian; I was a fairly sheltered one, trying to figure out what it meant to live for Christ in "the secular world." That fall the Toronto Blue Jays made the play-offs for the first time, and my friend invited me to one of the campus bars to watch a game.

Now, let me say that I'm not a teetotaler. I've never thought moderation a bad thing. But at that time in my life, I was uncomfortable going into such obviously "worldly" places. As we sat down and ordered her beer and my Coke, I mentioned my discomfort. Her response was truly a revelation to me. She looked me in the eye and said: "Dwight, we sinners need you in here more than those saints need you out there."

My friend reminded me of the selfishness of my desire for purity. I wanted holiness without relationship. By my efforts to achieve that purity, I had in effect rejected the message of Christmas.

From that moment, my whole notion of ministry changed completely, and I committed to going where Jesus went with his gospel and to embracing all that he embraced in his love. If that makes me unspiritual in the eyes of other people, then so be it—which leads me to my next point.

Second, Christmas means that God calls us to a discipleship of weakness.

When I was a bit younger and studying to be a youth

minister, I discovered some of the great evangelical writers on spirituality—A. W. Tozer, Andrew Murray, E. M. Bounds, and a few others—and began to hunger to know God as these men and women had. I began to get up at 5:30 every morning to read and pray. I asked God to show me his glory. I was sure that as I did this each day, I would become a spiritual man—a man of God.

I don't know if that has happened or not, but I do know what *didn't* happen. I expected that my relationship with God would become somehow effortless, that getting up to pray for two hours would be easy, and that resisting the temptations that haunt me would eventually come naturally. Instead, I continued to fall asleep praying. There were days when I simply didn't want to pray; it was just too much work. There were days when God felt nonexistent, though I knew he loved me and I wanted to love him more than anything else in my life. There were times when instead of praying I found myself yearning not for God, but for very *un*spiritual things. (Let me tell you, there's very little that's more guilt-inducing than preaching to a three-thousand-member church and trying to get thoughts of the girl in the balcony out of your head.) I was sure that there was something desperately wrong with me. I mean, we're either on-fire, hot-for-God, zealous-for-the-Lord-super-Christians, or we're complacent, lazy, dead-in-our-faith, spiritual deadbeats, right? Hot or cold? Black or white? And since there were times when I wasn't "on fire," and since my praying and doing right was more often than not a struggle, I assumed the worst.

And then, as part of my agonizing, I read Romans 8:26-27 (Phillips):

> The Spirit of God . . . helps us in our present limitations. For example, we do not know how to pray worthily as sons of God, but his Spirit within us is actually praying for us in those agonizing longings which never find words. And God who knows the

heart's secrets understands, of course, the Spirit's intention as he prays for those who love God. . . .

Here—sandwiched between Paul's declaration that there is "no condemnation" in Christ and his powerful pronouncement that as Christians we are "more than conquerors" in Christ—he tells us that we don't even know how to do the most elementary spiritual task: pray. And more, he tells us that that weakness is not necessarily a function of our sin or our spiritual laziness, but rather, simply a function of our context. We are weak, plain and simple, and the world we live in is broken. Sometimes this old world just gets in the way of knowing its Creator.

The Incarnation understands that. The Incarnation says our place of brokenness is where God chose to make his home. For those of us who would seek to be Christ's disciple, this is most encouraging. Doubt, questions—even ambivalence—are not necessarily signs of a lack of faith. Rather, they are functions of living in a world that is not yet all God wants it to be. God understands the limits of our frail humanity and made that frailty the starting point of his Incarnation. He knows our sinfulness, yes, but also our finiteness. And he knows that sin and finiteness *are not the same.*

For those of us who would be environmentalists, this frees us from the temptation of believing the world to be more "good" than it is. We don't have to believe it is free from limitations and brokenness to love it and advocate for it. We don't have to worship it as holy. But we can boldly assert that the Incarnation affirms that the world is, in spite of its brokenness, the Lord's. God has not abandoned it, and he doesn't expect us to, either. Instead, by the gift of the Spirit, Christ continues to embrace the frailty of creation, and to sanctify it, by offering his presence in it. And by his grace, he uses frail creation—and we humans in it—to unveil his glory.

You see, God doesn't need us, or his earth, to be perfect in order to use us. All God wants are people who will simply be available and follow where he leads—which leads me to my final point:

Third, Christmas means that God calls us to a discipleship of service.

The Incarnation tells us that we will not be measured by worldly standards of success. The measure of our discipleship will not be how well we avoided the difficulties of life, or our great feats of spirituality, like speaking in tongues or exorcising demons or raising the dead. First Corinthians 13 even tells us that we will not be evaluated on the basis of things like whether or not we give all our possessions to the poor. Trust me, as the public relations director for a group called Evangelicals for Social Action, that's a hard verse to hear!

No, the Incarnation provides us with an altogether different model of spirituality. The measure of our faith will be how well we follow Jesus *into* our world and how well we embrace those he embraced and offer them our very lives. Our text is simple: *"He was equal to God and yet became a slave. . . ."*

Anyone can give alms to the poor. Anyone can buy a hectare of rain forest, recycle, or buy environmentally friendly products. But will we follow Jesus? Will we be a friend—a neighbor—of the poor, and of the earth?

Who were his neighbors? He came as a poor man, was born on a trash heap, and lived among the weak and the outcast, the unsuspecting and the irreligious. Jesus did not feel compelled to win the powerful first and then hope for trickle-down evangelism. No. In fact, Jesus didn't feel compelled to win anyone. Rather, he went to the weak, powerless, and oppressed. He went to women, lepers, and traitors—all those his culture exploited and used—healing them and giving them a place to belong. He went to the exploiters and in his call to repentance offered them belonging, too. And he says to us, "Follow me." Will we?

Conclusion

This Christmas, we need Christians who will celebrate the Incarnation—Christians who will leap into our world with abandon—to celebrate the fact that in Christ, God refused to abandon us. We need to refuse to make our discipleship just about getting to heaven or even about being holy. We need to be unafraid to let God love us, and use us, as we are. And we need to offer ourselves to those the world despises—the losers of our world—to befriend the friendless, to love those who are hardest to love.

The community of Emmanuel—God *with* us—ought to be marked by a dissident, subversive character that refuses to define success in terms of power and influence, but that instead is marked by selflessness, generosity, and kindness—a community that responds lavishly to the needs it finds. Maybe then, when we are unwrapped by the world around us, we will be surprised to discover that we have shown them Jesus.

May it be so.

[This sermon was first preached on November 30, 1994, at the Eastern College Chapel, St. Davids, Pennsylvania.]

I Shop, Therefore I Am:
Wounded Hearts, Wounded Earth

Jim Wallis

Therefore I tell you, do not worry about your life, what you will eat or drink; or about your body, what you will wear. Is not life more important than food, and the body more important than clothes? Look at the birds of the air; they do not sow or reap or store away in barns, and yet your heavenly Father feeds them. Are you not much more valuable than they? Who of you by worrying can add a single hour to his life?

And why do you worry about clothes? See how the lilies of the field grow. They do not labor or spin. Yet I tell you that not even Solomon in all his splendor was dressed like one of these. If that is how God clothes the grass of the field, which is here today and tomorrow is thrown into the fire, will he not much more clothe you, O you of little faith? So do not worry, saying, "What shall we eat?" or "What shall we drink?" or "What shall we wear?" For the pagans run after all these things, and your heavenly Father knows that you need them. But seek first his kingdom and his righteousness, and all these things will be given to you as well.

—Matthew 6:25-33

The British Airways steward announced that the in-flight movie would be "Chariots of Fire." "Is that the only one?" I asked.

"We are also showing 'Gandhi'," he replied.

"Where do I have to sit to see it?" I responded.

"I'm sorry, sir, but 'Gandhi' is only showing in first class."
The irony seemed to escape him.

Air travel is mostly a middle- and upper-class mode of
transportation. On long journeys spent in planes, passenger
lounges, and shuttle buses, one can hear a good sampling of the
conversation among people of the more affluent classes. In
listening, I've discovered that the overwhelming majority of the
talk is about consumption: where we ate last night and where
we will eat tonight; which hotel we will be staying in; where we
went on our last vacation and where we plan to go on the next
one; where the best shopping can be found.

On a flight home several years ago, I found myself on an
airport shuttle bus with other travelers. Two handsome young
white couples were having a loud conversation about their
favorite restaurants around the world. Many of the rest of us
would have preferred not to listen, but the close quarters left
us no choice. Finally, one of them exclaimed in praise of his
favorite place, "It's just a wonderful restaurant—two can
spend three hundred dollars for dinner in your shorts!"

At my destinations, the conversation is much different, often
about survival: Where will our next meal come from? How can
we keep the rain out and the children dry? Where can we find
water clean enough to drink? Will we ever have any land to call
our own?

How can two worlds be so far apart?

Our Modern Credo

The credo of modern consumerism screamed at me from the
bumper sticker: "I Shop, Therefore I Am." This contemporary
version of Descartes's old maxim, "I think, therefore I am,"
momentarily took my breath away with its stark truthfulness
about our materialistic age. The same week I saw the bumper
sticker, another murder occurred in my neighborhood—this
time over basketball shoes.

In many cities across America, it has become quite common
for kids to shoot each other for fancy athletic shoes, leather

jackets, or some other desirable possession. The bumper sticker declaration of the central meaning of our time struck me as far more brutal than humorous, when at the bottom rungs of the consumer society, children of the inner cities are killing each other for a pair of sneakers.

A Culture of Consumers

Consumption is the thing that everyone, the rich and the poor and everyone in between, seems to care most about. Our culture has managed to commercialize (and trivialize) almost everything. Not only does consumption define the culture; materialism has become the culture in America. Our possessions have come to possess us, and we ourselves have become almost wholly objectified as consumers and markets by the scientists of Madison Avenue. The entirely economic definition of life that shapes our society, without question, has cheapened our human existence. The result is a culture that is losing its very soul.

The problem is not that the young people haven't learned our values; it's that they have. They can see beneath our social and religious platitudes to what we care about most. Our great cultural message comes through loud and clear: It is an affluent lifestyle that counts for success and happiness. Yet we sometimes seem startled when the young really take our consumer values to heart and lose their hearts in the process.

In truth, we have become an addicted society. Many of our psychological therapists and healers who work with substance abusers have concluded that the whole social context in which we live today is an addictive one. Drugs and alcohol are not our only addictions. In the inner city of Washington, D.C., the money that comes from drugs is another addiction leading to violence.

That addiction—the addiction to materialism—is fed every hour of every day in this society. And it is not only legal to feed that addiction; it is the whole purpose of the system. It is our reason for being as a people—to possess and consume.

The images dance before us every waking moment. They attract, allure, and create desire; they awaken the greed and covetousness of our worst selves. Our children are glued to the television screen, and the beat of incessant consumption pounds in their ears. At every level of the life cycle, our hopes and fears, vanities and insecurities, aspirations and appetites are carefully researched and mercilessly exploited. Our many addictions are systematically created, creatively cultivated, and constantly manipulated.

Everything has a sponsor now. Every moment of every day is brought to us by somebody who wants to sell us something—most of which is demonstrably harmful to us or useless for a meaningful and satisfying life. The beginning of consumer wisdom is to understand that we have become part of the merchandise. It is consumers that are now bought and sold.

Celebrities as Leaders

For the most part, America no longer celebrates leaders, only celebrities. What is a celebrity? A celebrity is somebody who wants to sell you something and get famous and rich by doing so.

The celebrity competition was stiff in the 1994 Super Bowl ads. There was Shaquille O'Neal rapping and slam-dunking for Reebok; Chevy Chase getting canceled again in a Doritos ad; Mike Ditka coaching the tired old football game between Bud and Bud Lite beer bottles; Michael Jordan and Larry Bird shooting baskets from outer space to sell Big Macs; Michael Jordan and Steve Martin selling Nikes (Michael has become our most promiscuous huckster); Bo Jackson running down a skyscraper for Lipton Tea; and, of course, Dan Quayle selling wavy Lay's Potato Chips.

I Shop, Therefore I Belong

Our shopping malls have become the temples, shrines, and communal centers of modern America. An advertisement on

D.C. Metro buses reads, "I was saved at Potomac Mills," and displays a large picture of a dollar bill. George Washington smiles down upon observers, presumably over the terrific savings he has just incurred while shopping at the large discount mall. Malls combine every conceivable kind of store with movies, restaurants, video arcades, exercise clubs, and, more recently, condominiums, so you never even have to leave home. The total-environment mall may be the best archetype of our advanced consumer culture.

Consumerism offers us its own sense of community. Magazine articles seriously suggest that a sign of global community is that we can travel all over the world and find the golden arches of McDonald's. Ads for Coca-Cola feature young people of every race and nation all singing in joyful chorus, with a bottle of Coke in every hand, while the now world-famous Coca-Cola signs rise over the misery and death of squatter camps and shantytowns around the globe.

The issue here is deeper than greed and selfishness. Material consumption—buying and possessing things—has become the primary way of belonging in America and around the world. If we can't buy, if we can't consume, we simply can't belong.

I once saw a newspaper column announcing a new, simulated car phone. For five dollars you can buy a piece of plastic that looks like a car phone. It doesn't work, but from outside your car in the parking lot, it looks like the real thing. The motivation for such a product isn't greed, it's belonging.

Perhaps our shared cultural values reflect the emptiness of our situation most of all. Television rules the popular culture, and advertising dominates television. Television has become the principal vehicle for promoting consumerism. It is the message of the medium. Consumption has become our highest social value and purpose. In fact, material consumption is the only universal form of social participation that Americans have left. Everything else has been either marginalized or completely co-opted by the frenzied desire for things.

Our Crisis of Values

Yes, we are suffering a crisis of values. However, the charge that values are lacking is normally addressed to those on the bottom of society, to inner-city youth and young perpetrators of street crime. We often hear political candidates speak of a criminal class that must be locked up. However, since the United States has more persons incarcerated in proportion to its population than any nation on earth, it might be time to ask why. Clearly, we are suffering from a profound erosion of moral values. But where does it come from?

Frustrated Desire

We simply must stop continually pumping the moral pollution of rampant consumerism into the heads and hearts of the young. As long as we continue to do so, we have no right to be shocked when they behave as selfish materialists. By creating the desire for affluence, then blocking its satisfaction, we are fueling a combustion engine of frustration and anger. We can no longer exclude whole communities from the economic mainstream, relegate them to the peripheries, tell them in a thousand ways that their labor and their lives are not needed, abandon their social context to disintegration and anarchy, and then be surprised when those communities erupt.

When there are no ethics at the top of a society, it's likely there will be none at the bottom either. Our urban children have inherited our values. The violent carnage of our inner cities is the underside of a consumer society that uses violence as entertainment. Looting is a crude shopping spree reflecting a system that loots and pollutes the rest of the world.

When the kids on the street during the Los Angeles riots said of looting, "Everyone was doing it," they didn't just mean their neighbors and friends. The savings-and-loan rip-off bankers are looters, too, as are the military contractors who always run over budget and the Wall Street inside traders, merger-makers, and takeover pirates.

Our Material World

At root, we might examine the reality of our material world: In our consumer culture, things have become far more important than people and creation. Indeed, people themselves have been turned into things to be used and abused in a society where everything and everyone is a commodity to be bought and sold. The commodification of human life is the moral framework upon which our materialistic system has been built. It is that whole system that inevitably produces the amorality we now suffer.

There is a biblical proverb that says, "Where there is no vision, the people perish" (Proverbs 29:18 KJV). This proverb can be translated in slightly different ways. Another translation says, "Where there is no prophecy the people cast off restraint" (RSV). The bitter meaning of that sentence has become painfully clear to me now, right in my own neighborhood. When vision is lacking, people quickly degenerate into their worst selves and begin behaving in violent and destructive ways.

Martin Luther King Jr. recognized the intimate connection between our materialism and all our other problems more than a quarter century ago, when he wrote in *Where Do We Go From Here?* that as a nation we must undergo a radical "revolution of values."

We must rapidly . . . shift from a "thing"-oriented society to a "person"-oriented society. When machines and computers, profit motives and property rights are considered more important than people, the giant triplets of racism, materialism, and militarism are incapable of being conquered.

Twenty-five years later, we have yet to address the spiritual crisis that our worship of things has produced, and we are reaping the consequences. Human creatures have become commodities. Bullets pierce the air of the inner city, creating a new kind of violent air pollution. The beauty of human cultures is being degraded by extinction or at least assimilation. And indeed, all of creation is unraveling. The artistry of the Maker is headed for the garbage dumps and landfills.

The Wounded Earth

The aboriginal leader took his food and walked some distance away from the small crowd that had assembled for lunch at a community site run by the indigenous people in western Australia. He sat alone on the ground and began to eat his meal. I followed the tribal elder out onto the dusty red earth, where he invited me to sit with him. We had been speaking earlier about the life of the community there, the projects the people were undertaking, and his determination to pass on a way of life to the young. Now he began to talk about what it means to be an Australian aborigine.

He reached down and put his hand on the ground beneath us. Then, putting his hand on his chest, he continued, "I can feel the earth in my bones, in my flesh, and in the blood moving through my body." Our lives depend on the earth, he told me, and we also must depend on each other. "That's why we share what we have with one another. There is no one here who goes without. We would not let that happen."

Earlier that morning, the Australian newspapers carried an image that was the exact opposite of what my aboriginal friend described. There on the front page was a picture of George Bush sitting in his golf cart and ordering American troops to the Persian Gulf over his mobile phone. The contrast between these two leaders could not have been more stark.

I was in the middle of Australia in August 1990, when Saddam Hussein's Iraqi army invaded Kuwait and sparked the chain of events that eventually led to the Gulf War. I stayed up very late one night in Australia to hear President Bush speak live to the American people in his first speech after the crisis began.

During the hour before his address, while I waited nervously, Australian television aired a documentary on the environment, specifically the growing dangers to the earth's ecosystem from global warming trends and pollution caused by the industrial world's massive dependence on fossil fuels, that is, oil. I then watched George Bush tell the American people that we must be prepared to go to war to protect the supply of oil. Nothing less was at stake, said the president, than "our way of life."

It was a very vivid and frightening picture, in the middle of the night and halfway around the world, of my own nation—addicted to a way of life that is slowly killing us. In all the coverage and commentary about this crisis over oil, few ever really asked the most important question: What does the oil fuel?

The Economic Earth

What the oil fuels is a global economic system of massive consumption at the top and massive misery at the bottom, a system we know is doing incalculable damage to the natural order in which we live. Consuming a grossly disproportionate share of the world's resources, the West suffocates in its own affluence, while even within the wealthy nations, more and more people are abandoned to poverty. The United States, with only 6 percent of the world's population, still consumes 35 percent of the earth's resources. And the distribution of those resources within the United States has become visibly obscene.

The world economic order is not only unjust, it is also unstable, as the Gulf War demonstrated. Even getting rid of the Saddam Husseins does not remove the underlying instability in the Middle East. The truth is that the West itself has helped to create the situation in which we now find ourselves. Western colonialism and the thirst for oil drew up the map of the Middle East to the point even of carving out the borders of all the Arab states embroiled in present-day conflicts.

Kuwait and Saudi Arabia were established to ensure a continual supply of cheap oil for the West. Oil-rich states are run by corrupt and brutal elites who abandon their own people, crush all opposition, fight among themselves for wealth and power, live in incredible opulence, and invest their untold fortunes in the West, while Arab masses live in poverty and resentment. The feudal oil sheiks have proven quite willing to cut favorable political deals with their colonial benefactors, humiliating Arab pride and inciting Arab nationalism.

And sometimes, as in the case of Saddam Hussein, the greed and ambition get out of control and threaten the oil contract, which is the bottom line of the relationship to the West. The West arms all the Middle Eastern states (and has thus flooded the entire region with sophisticated weaponry), plays them off against one another, generally ignores their abuses (including Iraq's many past horrors), changes alliances as quickly as shifting desert sands, and seeks to manage events with no consistent principle except our insatiable thirst for oil. The United States' commitment to restore a Kuwaiti royal family that has suppressed every democratic impulse in that country— and to defend a Saudi monarchy with one of the more dismal human rights records in the world suggests that we are making the world safe more for feudalism and gas guzzling than for democracy.

The High Price of Oil

Clearly, what the United States cared most about during the Gulf crisis was oil. The United States was willing to pay a high price to secure continued access to oil on our terms. The price of the Gulf War included over a hundred American lives and as many as one hundred thousand Iraqi soldiers and civilian casualties. The price included risking the potential use of chemical warfare and even tactical nuclear weapons.

The genuine fear and concern of many Americans over the prospect of losing loved ones in the sands of the Arabian Peninsula was caused by something far deeper than a so-called madman in Iraq; it was the direct consequence of "reaping what we have sown." The easy success of the war quickly covered over the deeper questions that it had begun to raise.

"The bugle from the Middle East," wrote columnist Ellen Goodman, "sounds an unhappy wake-up call." We are confronted with soul-searching questions that simply will not go away. What are we most willing to sacrifice—a way of life based on massive overconsumption, or the lives of young Americans and other peoples it may take to keep it going? How many cents on a gallon of gas are equal to the human cost of so many potential deaths? What are we ready to risk—changes in our lifestyle or the prospect of endless future confrontations?

Are we ready to make the critical choices to opt for less dependence on oil, for energy conservation, and for the shift to safer, more reliable, and renewable sources of fuel for the sake of the earth and our children? Are we prepared to begin a serious dialogue about what a more equitable and sustainable global economy might look like? Or are we prepared to again bomb the children of Baghdad, or somewhere else, if necessary, to protect "our way of life"?

Farmer and poet Wendell Berry reflected at the end of the Gulf War:

> If we want to be at peace, we will have to waste less, spend less, use less, want less, need less. The most alarming sign of the state of our society now is that our leaders have the courage to sacrifice the lives of our young people in war, but have not the courage to tell us that we must be less greedy and less wasteful.

The Cry of the Heart

Around our world, we see the pain and violence of life at the bottom of a global economy. But we can also see the problem at suburban malls, where the human heart is slowly dying because of our failure to recognize that we were created for more than consumption. At the upper end of the world's hierarchical chasms, the affluent drown in loneliness and anxiety, and their children wander aimlessly in a society in which there is always more to buy but nowhere to find meaning. These are the spiritual consequences of our sin—we are separated from God, from one another, and from the earth. The anxiety and despair of affluent cultures is a direct result of their unjust relationship to impoverished people and nations. Again, the principle holds true: We are inexorably linked together.

Underneath the noisy chaos of our consumer culture, the constant rush of media images that define our reality, and the relentless pressure of a lifestyle that demands our very souls, do we even hear the cry of the poor? And beneath *their* cry, can we hear the cry of creation *itself*? At the deepest level, can we even hear the cry of our own hearts?

The conservatives say the problem is a breakdown of values; the liberals say the cause is poverty. They are both right and both wrong. Our value structures have broken down. The most basic understandings of simple decency and respect can no longer be taken for granted. Mary Sarton, introducing John LeCarré's *The Russia House*, says, "One must think like a hero to behave like a merely decent human being." We have entered an amoral era, where notions of right and wrong, which were once commonly held assumptions, are gradually slipping away.

All of life has been reduced to consumption. We sacrifice our souls for the mirage of glittering images, and all we get is a mouthful of sand. We have run after mirages in the desert, and now the desert is in us.

Perhaps now, as never before, the words of Jesus that we read earlier can bring refreshing streams of living water to our spiritual deserts. If we will but listen to his teaching and embrace the values of the kingdom, we can be healed of the sins that are tearing us apart.

In such gospel wisdom is the beginning of the more relaxed and balanced perspective we need to put material things back in their proper place and to restore the rightful priority of human life, relationships, and the integrity of the whole created order.

Another bumper sticker I've seen is the one that reads, "Live Simply, So Others May Simply Live." That slogan gets close to the heart of things. We are all connected. As long as some can talk only about their materialism, others can talk only about their survival. We must stop being distressed at the loss of rain forests (as distressing as that is) and start repenting of what is happening in our malls and even in our homes. If we are going to point a finger at population problems abroad, we must allow that finger to point at the problems of *our own* possessions and pleasure.

One of the most urgently needed values in our land today is

compassion. Compassion means a radical empathy for all those who suffer under present arrangements. This means suffering in all its forms, including both the oppression of the world's poor and marginalized majority, and the spiritual and psychological disintegration of the affluent minority because of that very oppression.

Choosing to live by oppressive values is one of the most decisive causes of both the alienation of the affluent and the self-destruction of the poor, as is dramatically illustrated in the violent inner-city neighborhoods of America. We now witness the tragic irony of growing numbers of people in the middle classes being gripped with the recessionary fear of falling down the social ladder while simultaneously experiencing the personal and family consequences of the empty and competitive values of a materialistic society. We are afraid of losing what is already killing us.

These lifestyle values have turned people into objects. *People*—created in the glorious image of the Creator God—have been reduced to things. Our greed and sin have surely contributed to the unraveling of families in our inner cities, while around the world, whole cultures are being lost as they move to the cities for their share of "the good life." This corruption of God's image, this loss of human cultural diversity, is surely an affront to the Creator who wants the glories of his human creation to be known. Finally, our demands for more and more possessions and conveniences have squandered the beauty, richness, and fruitfulness of the nonhuman creation.

We *must* change. Both planet and people are crying out for a change.

The Cost of Change

The creation and all its abundance is good. It is meant to be both shared and enjoyed. But our overconsumption has damaged creation, our materialism has corrupted our hearts, and injustice has wounded our souls. The violence we do to one another, either through unjust structures of international trade and finance or through street crime, is the consequence of our sin. And change will be costly.

We need a citizens' movement against overconsumption. The best way to resist the materialistic values of a consumer society is simply to withdraw our participation from them and to find alternative ways to live that are more creative, healthy, life-giving, and even fun. That will not be an easy task, but it is possible, especially with the support and energy that can be generated by people doing it together. It is already occurring in diverse places, where the excesses of affluence, concern for the environment, and a desire for justice have created both disaffection and a hunger for new patterns of resource use. People are finding new ways to meet their legitimate needs, ways that don't destroy the earth, their global neighbors, their children's moral characters, and their own humanity in the process.

What better place to start than right here in our own church? We are the community of Christ trying to demonstrate the values of a different kingdom to a world that is languishing in its own twisted values. Can we live in such a way that the world will sit up and take notice? Will they see by our rejection of a lifestyle that holds them in bondage that there *is* hope? Can we be a people who "seek first his kingdom and his righteousness" (Matthew 6:33)? The world is literally dying to see us in action.

Alcoholics Anonymous and related groups for various other substance abuses have become a spiritual home and haven for many recovering people. As a recovering friend of mine puts it, "A.A. is not for people who want to keep from going to hell, but for those who have already been there." The standard introduction of a member goes like this: "Hi, my name is Bill, and I'm an alcoholic." And the whole group responds with acceptance, "Hi, Bill!"

Perhaps we need to learn from the successful principles of Alcoholics Anonymous and have meetings that begin, "Hi, my name is Bill, and I am a materialistic overconsumer." It sounds funny, of course, but acceptance of our mutual problem would make it possible for the process of healing and recovery to begin. The issues involved in our destructive overconsumption are more than political; they go to the spiritual core of our identities and needs.

Out of that spiritual transformation, a citizens' boycott of wasteful and destructive consumerism could, over time, have a profound effect in reshaping the marketplace and altering the very values of the culture. The thing Madison Avenue most fears is that people will stop listening to its mindless and manipulative advertising. Why don't we try it? Just turn it off. Let them ramble on in their trivialities and falsehoods; we won't be paying attention.

We simply cannot go on living as we do, consuming as we please, profiting as much as we can, and running the economy as we are, while using the money that is left over to "help the poor." There is never "enough" left over, and the poor will continue to lose.

It is we who have to change, and it is our patterns and institutions that must be transformed. There is much work to be done and many jobs to be created to bring us the things we all need—education, health, energy efficiency, a safe and restored environment, healthy food, good roads, strong bridges, easier and cleaner transportation, affordable housing, stable families, and vital communities.

Such things will be helped by a combination of solid values and sound social policy. And it will require a number of fundamental shifts—from unlimited growth to a sustainable society, from endlessly consuming goods to revaluing social goods, from the ethic of competition to an ethic of community. Such shifts will not be easy, nor will they be without cost. But the cost of not making the changes will be even greater.

Appendix A

More Sermon Ideas

The Best Preaching on Earth is a collection of sermons provided to give you some starter ideas for incorporating creation care into the preaching and teaching ministry of your church. A few additional ideas are gathered in this appendix.

Whenever you are preaching on sin, it would be helpful, as well as instructive, to start including environmental destruction, greed, and waste to illustrate the reality of sin. We can hope the days are gone when the preacher lists dancing, movies, and card playing as cardinal sins. Nonetheless, sin still thrives in our culture. Modern people need to be challenged to care for creation, and the necessary first step is repentance for what we have done.

Whenever you are preaching on stewardship, as many of us do each fall, you could incorporate reflections on the environment. The standard stewardship sermon deals with finances, sometimes the use of our time or talents. However, the Bible teaches that everything belongs to God. "The earth is the LORD'S," says Psalm 24:1. The pastor needs to lead his or her congregation to consider the lordship of Jesus Christ in absolutely every area of life!

Additional ideas for sermon series or single sermons on creation care follow.

Sermon Series
Option One: "The Creator God"
Purpose: To ground the congregation in a doctrine of God as it relates to the creation.

The God of Power (Genesis 1:1). Who is this God who can create something out of nothing? What could God's power accomplish in my life?

The God of Goodness (Genesis 1:4,10,12,18,21,25,31: "It was good"). How does the creation display the goodness of God? What thanks will I give for his goodness in my life?

The God of Wisdom (Psalm 104:24). How does God's creation reflect his wisdom? What wisdom do I need for my life today?

The God Who Is Worthy (Revelation 5:13; Psalm 104:31). What does it mean to worship the Creator? Join with all creation in lifting voices of praise!

Option Two: "The Christ of Creation"
Purpose: To study the relationship of the Lord Jesus Christ to the creation.

Text for the series: Colossians 1:15-23. Please note the frequent use of the word "all" in the passage.

Christ the Creator (v. 16: "all things were created"; also John 1:1-4). Jesus was present at creation and made all things.

Christ the Sustainer (v. 17: "in him all things hold together"). Jesus holds this world together (sustains it) by his power (Hebrews 1:3).

Christ the Ruler (v. 18: "in everything . . . the supremacy"; see also vv. 16-17). Jesus continues to rule over all creation.

Christ the Redeemer (v. 20: "reconcile to himself all things"). The work of Christ on the cross is so powerful that its effects extend to all creation (Romans 8:19-22).

Option Three: "God Gave Them Voices"
Purpose: To help your congregation discover the biblical teaching that all creation has a voice that it can use to praise God (Psalm 96:11-13). Here is an option for a series to take your

congregation through an investigation of these "voices." With special attention to the musical element of your services during this series, a very effective worship experience could be planned.

The First Voices (Job 38:4-7, esp. v. 7). Imagine what it was like when the chorus first began. What reasons did they have for praising God? When did I first begin to praise God? What do I still have to learn?

The Song Goes On (Psalm 96:11-13). Daily and in every place, all creation praises God. For sermon illustrations, share information on the voices in creation: birds, insects, whales, and so forth. What is your song to the Creator? Is it old and worn out or fresh and inspiring (Psalm 40:3)?

The Sin That Silences (Romans 8:19-22). The first two sermons of this series are based on uplifting passages. Romans 8 conveys a very different tone! Here the creation "groans." What is sin doing to our planet? What or who is the solution?

God, Give Us Voices to Praise You! (Psalm 96:1-3). The whole earth is praising God. What does it take to wake up the human creation to praise the Creator? What does it mean to worship God?

Quotable quote: "Many people go through life as though they were wearing blinders or were sleepwalking. Their eyes are open, yet they may see nothing of their wild associates on this planet. Their ears, attuned to motor cars and traffic, seldom catch the music of nature—the singing of birds, frogs or crickets—or the wind. . . . They may know business trends or politics, yet haven't the faintest idea of what makes the natural world tick" (Roger Tory Peterson, speech at Bloomsburg University, quoted in *Time*, June 17, 1985). Roger Tory Peterson has written many field guides for nature study and is credited with making the natural world more accessible for millions of people around the world.

Option Four: "Gardening with God"

Purpose: To study the relationship between humans and the Garden of Eden. God created the world and placed humans in a

Garden. What was the Garden like? What went wrong there? How can we get back to the Garden?

The Garden of God (Genesis 1:27—2:25). What was God's original plan for humans in the Garden? What were the blessings? What were the responsibilities?

The Garden and Sin (Genesis 3). What happened when sin entered the Garden? Focus on the disruption of all relationships: with self, with other humans, with nature, and with God.

The Garden and Christ (John 15:1-17). Investigate the impact of "abiding" in Christ on these broken relationships. (Another pertinent text: Christ in the Garden of Gethsemane, Matthew 26:36-46).

The Garden of Hope (Revelation 22:1-5). Look forward to the new Garden and the healing that will happen there.

Recommended resource: Vera Shaw's *Thorns in the Garden Planet* (Nelson, 1993), a good devotional book with plenty of discussion questions.

Option Five: "The Lord God Made Them All"

Purpose: In 1 Kings 4:33-34, we read that King Solomon taught about the plants and animals. The purpose of this sermon series is to learn some big lessons from some small creatures. These sermons will require that you "do your homework" in natural history. Use a Bible encyclopedia or concordance to look up references to different plants and animals.

Study the Ant (Proverbs 6:6). What lessons can be learned from the ants? Examples: (1) The weak can be strong. Tiny as they are, ants can drag objects that weigh two or three times their own body weight. Compare that with human ability and body weight. (2) Communication is important. Ants "talk" by touching feelers. Scientists have compiled an ant "dictionary" of these communications. (3) Hard work is important.

Watch the Birds (Jeremiah 8:6-7). This text seems to imply that birds know more about obedience to God than the human creation. How good are we at following in the paths of God?

Consider the Lilies (Matthew 6:28-34). Why does Jesus

encourage the disciples to give their attention to the lilies? What will they teach us?

Meditate on Mortals (Psalm 8:3-5). In a world of glorious creations, consider the splendor of the human creation!

Recommended Resources

Paul Brand and Philip Yancey, *In His Image* and *Fearfully and Wonderfully Made.* These two books reveal the marvels of the human creation.

G. S. Cansdale, *All the Animals of the Bible Lands* (Zondervan, 1970).

F. Nigel Hepper, *Baker Encyclopedia of Bible Plants* (Baker, 1992).

Haddon Robinson, "Proverbial Pests," *Christianity Today,* April 27, 1992.

Single Sermons

What Will I Leave Behind?

Text: Proverbs 13:22: "A good man leaves an inheritance for his children's children."

Central Idea: It is an act of righteousness to make sure that we curb our excesses in order to share valuable resources with our grandchildren.

Sermon Content: It would seem that we are leaving very little behind (except a mountain of trash) and are fast running out of resources. To act in this way is (1) silly, (2) selfish, and (3) sinful. Suggest some practical actions, such as "reduce, reuse, recycle" *and* "repent, rethink, rejoice" (Hodgson and Sider in W. Dayton Roberts, *Patching God's Garment,* p. 119).

Let There Be Praise

Text: Psalm 148.

Central Idea: All creation raises a symphony of praise to God. In this age of environmental destruction, the music of creation is being silenced.

Sermon Content: (1) Some Creatures Sing. Mention the many voices of creation: birds, insects, whales, and so forth. (2)

Some Creatures Shout. The focus here could be the grandeur of human music and its invaluable place in our lives. (3) Some Creatures Are Silent. Notice Psalm 148:5,13: "Let them praise." Are we letting creation praise its Creator? Are we standing in the way? We work hard at making sure that missionaries have the opportunity to help other cultures praise their Maker. We plan our worship services to make sure the quality is glorifying to God. What are we doing to our planet? Perhaps we are interfering with the worship.

Illustration: How would a teenager feel if her favorite radio station went off the air? How would you feel if someone destroyed your son's trumpet (or other favorite instrument)? Can we imagine how God might react to the loss of species that praise him? The story of Noah shows us God's desire to save all life.

A Bull in the Neighborhood

Text: Exodus 21:28-32.

Central Idea: Good neighbors do not harm others.

Sermon Content: The Exodus text does not paint a pretty picture, but the implications are far-reaching in this age of toxins and environmental hazards. We are not allowed to harm our neighbors. Jesus commanded his disciples to love their neighbors as themselves (Matthew 22:39). Many other Scripture passages help define what it means to be a good neighbor. In this modern day, we need to rethink what it means to be a good neighbor. Too often, it is the poor who pay the price of our pollution. Love requires that we understand the human impact of our refuse and waste.

Illustration: Contact your local environmental protection agency or regional church office to see whether there are any toxic sites in your area. In some areas, local churches are fighting a battle against landfills or incinerators in their "backyards."

A Message for a Movement

Text: Acts 17:16-34: "The God who made the world and everything in it is the Lord of heaven and earth" (v. 24).

Central Idea: Paul gives the church an example of how to take the gospel to spiritually hungry people who do not know God.

Sermon Content: Many people involved in the environmental movement are showing their hunger for God. Some are involved in various religions, Native American spirituality, and so forth. These people understand that the answers to today's environmental problems are spiritual. This is a great evangelistic opportunity for the church. We can declare the truth of the God they seek. What then is the message for these hungry people?

(1) God is believable. Paul affirms the Athenians for their spiritual interests (v. 22) but says there is more. God can be known as the Creator (v. 24). We too can affirm the yearnings of some environmentalists while declaring the truth about God. (2) God is beyond us. Paul challenges the Athenian desire to spiritualize inanimate objects (vv. 24-25). Some modern spiritualities tend to equate God with life in general. We must be careful to stress the transcendence of God. (3) God is beside us. Although transcendent, God is not aloof (vv. 27-28). God is not a part of creation, but he does sustain it.

Illustration: "The environmental movement is an ethic looking for a religion—indeed, a religion looking for God," writes Loren Wilkinson, Regent College, Vancouver, British Columbia.

Things Too Wonderful

Text: Job 38—42, esp. 42:1-4.

Central Idea: In the midst of Job's deep suffering, God speaks to him of the wild majesty of the creation.

Sermon Content: After all that Job had suffered, it is interesting to note that God's "answer" is a poetic description of the creation. Study the passage for your own conclusions, but God may be making these points:

(1) We need a focus. Suffering tends to turn us inward and preoccupy us with personal concerns. Creation gives us the "big picture."

(2) We need humility. God used the majesty of creation to put

Job in his proper context. God has his own ways and plans (42:2).

(3) We need God more than we need anything else, even healing (42:5).

Illustration: "I have been determined in captivity, and still am determined, to convert this experience into something that will be useful and good for other people. I think that's the way to approach suffering. It seems to me that Christianity doesn't in any way lessen suffering. What it does is enable you to take it, to face it, to work through it, and eventually to convert it" (Terry Waite, former Beirut hostage, in *Church Times,* December 27, 1991).

Appendix B

What Is the Evangelical Environmental Network?

• A *fellowship* of Christians who know the time has come for human *creatures* to honor the *Creator* and care for his good and glorious *creation*.

• An *association* of those committed to making creation care a part of faithful discipleship and to praying, planning, and strategizing toward this goal.

Purpose: The Evangelical Environmental Network (EEN) seeks to nurture a biblically grounded, scientifically informed environmental movement within the evangelical community that understands the urgency of the global crisis and realizes that environmental concern and action are essential to Christian belief and discipleship.

Programs and Resources: The Network oversees a variety of programs and develops resources that will lay the groundwork for a movement of creation care and foster leadership to accomplish this goal. Following is a partial listing.

Conferences

Conferences for pastors, parachurch organizations, and Christian leaders are organized to address creation care from a biblical framework. This includes the Christian Environmental Council, a "think tank" of leaders who meet annually to promote a scriptural understanding of environmental issues.

The Declaration

This document, drafted by theologians, scientists, and professors, calls the evangelical community to embrace a commitment to the earth as an expression of the lordship of Jesus Christ. Hundreds of leaders have been invited to sign the declaration. The invitation is extended to you as well. Write for your copy of the Declaration.

Curriculum

The EEN works with Christian colleges and seminaries to encourage them to adopt an interdisciplinary approach to including creation care in their educational programs.

Public Policy Resources

Writers are commissioned to produce materials in the area of environmental policy and biblical faith.

Church Kits

Resources are available for the church through the EEN that provide ideas and information for Bible study, worship, and so forth. These kits are also practical for camps, schools, and the like.

A Magazine

In a partnership effort, the EEN publishes a magazine, *Green Cross*. This resource is a prophetic and inspirational voice for biblical people who seek to care for creation. Write for a sample copy.

The Evangelical Environmental Network has adopted the Lausanne Covenant as its statement of faith. The statement was initiated by Evangelicals for Social Action, Inc., and World Vision and is a collaborative effort with the National Religious Partnership for the Environment, which includes Jews, Catholics, and mainline Protestants.

For more information about the Network or to inquire about any of the above mentioned resources, please write or call:

The Evangelical Environmental Network
10 East Lancaster Avenue
Wynnewood, PA 19096
Telephone: 610/645-9392; 800/261-7741
Fax: 610/649-8090
Email: een@esa.mhs.compuserve.com

p.65 LA in Seattle - disconnecting gospel from creation.
accusations of New Age